MW01488838

Translator Self-Training German

Practical Course in Technical Translation

Morry Sofer

Schreiber Publishing
Rockville, Maryland

Acknowledgment: Section 2, Assignment 4, and Section 3, Assignment 4, are used with the kind permission of the World Bank.

Library of Congress Control Number: 00-135100
ISBN 1-887563-62-8

Printed in the U.S.A. by Schreiber Publishing, PO Box 4193, Rockville, Maryland 20849
301-424-7737   1-800-822-3213
www.schreibernet.com

Preface

This practical course is for anyone who would like to pursue technical translation in German and English, in such areas as legal, medical, financial or other kinds of non-literary documents (literary translation is a different discipline from technical).

The course is based on the practical experience of a major translation company which has been translating—routinely and successfully—German-into-English and English-into-German documents in all technical areas for almost twenty years. The assignments in this book are taken from real-life documents which were translated by this company, with names and other information changed in some cases to protect proprietary information.

This book grew out of a correspondence course offered about ten years ago, which became a three-ring binder program for translator's self-training five years ago. During those five years, hundreds of translators have used this program each year, and many have offered unsolicited praise for this program, letting us know that it has improved their translation skills, and in more than a few cases helped the user pass accreditation or certification tests for such organizations as the American Translators Association (ATA).

Nothing sharpens translation skills more than the actual act of translating. But one needs an entry point, either into the technical translation field in general, or into new areas of translation, if one has already been doing one kind of technical translation, such as legal. This course provides the entry point.

We at Schreiber Publishing take a personal interest in translators in all languages and subjects, and are always happy to hear from you.

Enjoy the course!

Morry Sofer

Table of Contents

SECTION 1. GENERAL

INTRODUCTION

Welcome to *Schreiber's* **Translator Self-Training Program**. We are very pleased you selected this program, which has been in use since 1992. It has helped aspiring translators around the country get their start in this exciting field, while assisting practicing translators in improving their translation skills. Translation is one of the fastest growing professions in today's world, as different languages and cultures are coming closer together every day. Whether you wish to pursue translation full-time or as a sideline, you will find it to be a highly challenging and quite profitable occupation. The purpose of the following exercises is to help you improve your skills as a German-into-English translator.

This program is designed to help you work at your own pace and gain experience through translation practice assignments. These assignments, excerpted from actual translation jobs, were selected to help you determine your own level of comfort and expertise, so that you may go on from there to choose the type of translation work you might like to pursue.

To derive the maximum benefit from these texts, you should carefully read the General Comments, the guidelines, and the specific notes which discuss each assignment. Every comment and every guideline represents years of experience in professional translation work. By carefully following this program, you will be able to achieve *in just a few days* what has taken others years to learn. You will be guided through many of the pitfalls of translation, taught how to avoid them, shown shortcuts in accomplishing a complex piece of translation work, and be given the benefit of comments designed to show you how to produce a translation acceptable to major clients such as government, industry, the legal world, and many more.

Before you read further, we strongly urge you to read Appendix A : Requisites for Professional Translators, and Appendix B : Translation Techniques.

The above-listed appendices will give you a good overview of how translation work is to be approached and practiced. Try to keep the contents of these chapters in mind as you translate the following assignments.

You are presented with four different texts, which, for most people, represent an increasing level of difficulty (although if you happen to be a lawyer, for example, it is possible that you will find the second assignment the easiest of the four). They are:
   1. **General**
   2. **Legal**
   3. **Chemical/Medical**
   4. **Business/Finance**

At a minimum, you may want to do the first and second assignments. Those two represent a vast body of material which is being translated in the United States on a regular basis, but which does not require a highly specialized vocabulary or technical background. The third assignment requires access to chemical and medical terminology, which can be managed by any intelligent translator. The fourth assignment should be approached with caution. Here one must have an understanding of the world of finance, which not all of us do. For your own self-assessment, you may want to try it (since we provide you with the translation, you can compare the results and see for yourself how you did). But if you find it too difficult, don't be discouraged. It is clearly not for everyone.

We hope you enjoy working with these texts, and we urge you to please be patient with yourself. One does not become an accomplished translator overnight. To learn, one must make mistakes. If your heart is in it, and if you love the challenge of working with two languages you happen to know well, then you are sure to get a great deal out of this program.

A Word about German Translation

German is one of the leading languages of European culture, scholarship, science and technology. A great deal of technical, scientific and legal documentation is generated in Germany and translated in the United States. At the same time, similar English-language documentation is regularly being translated into German. There are no exact statistics on this subject, but it is safe to assume that along with Spanish, Japanese, Russian and French, German is one of the top five most frequently translated languages in the United States.

Many American college students choose German for their foreign language requirement, or even major in this language. From all indications, given the popularity of the German language and the continued economic and cultural importance of Germany, German should continue to play a significant role on the international scene in the next century.

This means that developing one's skills as a German-into-English or English-into-German translator is time well spent. The United States and Germany continue to interact in all areas of commerce, science and technology. Documentation and literature flow between the two countries and between the U.S. and other German-speaking countries in a steady stream and in both directions. As the global village becomes more of a reality with every passing day, the interaction between German and English intensifies, and requires an ever-growing volume of translation in real time.

Some maintain that in time English will replace other languages such as German, Spanish, French etc. and will become the one language used by everyone in all international activities. Such claims were made in the past - in the time of the Roman Empire, for example. The fact remains, however, that at any given time in history there were always multiple cultural centers in the world, and even here in the United States, where English has been the dominant language for at least two centuries, other languages are gaining importance, and cultural pluralism, rather than disappearing, is flourishing.

The following exercises are designed to help you achieve a worthy and profitable goal - becoming an expert in improving communications between two of the world's major cultures and tongues - English and German.

The following comments are offered with two purposes in mind: the immediate purpose is to help you with the assignments. The long-term purpose is to serve as reference material for actual translation work. Keep them for future use.

A reminder:
The "source language" is the language you translate from.
The "target language" is the language you translate into.

Every language has its own "personality," so to speak. When you translate, pretend you are two different persons - a "German Person" and an "English Person." The German Person reads the original German text, and becomes familiar with it. The German Person then turns to the English Person, and says to him/her, **"Okay, now it's your turn to say the same thing your way."** Now the English Person takes over, and starts writing the same text in English. You will be constantly switching back and forth between the German and the English Persons, as the first checks the German word, phrase, sentence structure, and then the second thinks in English and comes up with the right equivalents. Here are some of the main language issues you will have to deal with:

Clarity

We each have our own personal style of expressing ourselves - in any language. Some people make their point clearly and succinctly, while others use more words than necessary, including esoteric words, to make their point. The same holds true in translation. You can translate the phrase, "Morgenstund hat Gold im Mund," as "The early bird catches the worm," or you could also translate it correctly as, "Those who rise early in the morning will increase their fortune." In the first instance, only six words were used; in the second, eleven. Most of the time, the first type of translation is better, because it is simpler and more readily understandable. Make it your point to pursue simplicity whenever possible.

Consistency

Most of the time, if you start out translating the word "Haus" as "house," stick to "house," and don't start suddenly shifting to "building," or vice versa. The reader may become confused, wondering why the word suddenly changed. Generally in English, building is bigger than house, and one may wonder whether the dimensions of that particular structure might have changed. If you are familiar with word-processing you know how easy it is to do a "global search and replace" throughout the text, so that if halfway into the document you decide that "building" is better than "house," then go back to the beginning and do a global change, replacing the word "house" with "building."

Sentence Structure

It is difficult, yet very important, to ensure that sentence structure is correct and makes sense, yet still retains the flavor of the original text, particularly if this is written in a flowery, elaborate, or otherwise unique style. This fine line is achieved mainly through practice, but it is definitely helpful to read the original several times before even beginning the translation process in order to gain a good idea of the author's style.

It is not necessary to follow the structure of a sentence literally. A run-on sentence which may make sense in one language may not make sense in the other, and therefore should be divided into two sentences (or more). The converse is also true. You should also avoid being too literal when it comes to word order, or your text will sound stilted, awkward, and artificial. You will need to rely on your own good writing skills in determining the most sensible word order and punctuation so that your translation flows smoothly.

Format

Format should be followed as closely as possible. Ideally, every page of translation should look exactly like the corresponding page of the original, except, of course, for the language. There is a very practical reason for this. It helps the reader, who may or may not know the source language, compare the two texts, make sure all the parts are there, and check a particular word or phrase in the source text. This, however, is not always possible, since a page of translation at times is longer than the same page in the source language. Nevertheless, every effort should be made to keep the format as similar as possible to the original.

Terminology

The use of the right terminology is critical in any translation, especially in technical subjects. Here the right kind of dictionaries and reference literature becomes very critical. Keep in mind, however, that dictionaries, no matter how good, are never complete, and do not provide all the answers. The other source of information is people who work in the field the particular translation covers. Their input is often more valuable than that of the dictionary, since they are the ones who work in the field and represent the potential readers of your translation.

The first thing to keep in mind about terminology - as was discussed before - is consistency. If you translate a word a certain way, do not change in the middle of the text to another synonym of the same word, even though it may be accurate. This will throw the reader off. The second thing is to make sure you are using the right terms, rather than trying to approximate them. Keep a list of those terms to maintain consistency throughout the document, and also for future use. If you continue to translate in the same technical field, these lists will become your most valuable translation tool.

Numbers

The use of commas and periods is reversed in numbers over 1000 (1.000 in German becomes

1,000 in English), and in decimals (0,5 in German, becomes 0.5 in English). This is one example of cultural differences which must be closely observed.

Punctuation

Quotation marks are appropriate in English, but this is not always so in German. Semicolons have their place in both languages, but not necessarily in the same places. These are just a few examples of how even a highly accurate translation will not always mirror its original text. You will often be called upon to be the judge, which involves a combination of excellent writing skills, knowledge of rules of grammar and punctuation, plus common sense.

Errors in the Source Text

Sometimes you will find that the original has errors, such as a misspelling where it is clear by the context that the author intended to say "der" and not "de," or the sequence in a series of numbered clauses is wrong, or a name that has been in upper case letters suddenly appears as lower case, for no apparent reason. You can do a number of things in situations such as these. You can go ahead and make the correction and leave it at that. You can translate the text as is, and use the term [sic] after the error, to alert the reader. Or you can make a translator's note on a separate sheet of paper. Ultimately, the client will have to decide what to do with it.

Untranslatable Words or Terms

You may run into a word, a term or a phrase which cannot be translated, or which should be left in the original language (such as, for instance, "Ersatz"). If there is a need to explain it, it can be done in a footnote or in parentheses (or brackets, which makes it clearer that the bracketed text is not part of the original) following the word (Ersatz [serving as a substitute, not the real item]). As a general rule, however, it is best not to burden your translation with footnotes or parenthetic or bracketed text.

In Conclusion

The above notes are by no means exhaustive. They do not cover all the issues facing a translator. Language is not mathematics. Keep this in mind, and do the best translation job you possibly can.

1. We are providing you with a German text and an English translation of that same text. Pretend you don't have the English translation. If you read it before you do the assignment, you will not be able to do an honest job, and you will not derive the benefit of learning from your own mistakes.

2. Read the German text once for general comprehension. Underline any difficult words or passages.

3. As you start the translation process by reading the text for the first time (see 2., above), keep track of time, so that when you finish you will know how long it took you to translate the text. This is very critical, because you want to increase your translation speed as you go along. The rule is simple: The more words you translate per hour, the more money you will make. A very low hourly word-count can earn you less than minimum wage, which is not at all desirable. (Note: The hours indicated at the top right hand corner for each assignment include two numbers. The first is for beginners while the second number is for an experienced translator. Therefore, an assignment that would take a beginner 5-7 hours to complete might take an experienced translator 2 hours. The timeframe includes research, draft, and final copy.)

4. Read it again. This time make a list of difficult words, and make any notes regarding things you need to clarify about the text (e.g., look up something in an encyclopedia to better understand some concept or piece of information).

5. Try to determine which dictionaries and reference books you need for this assignment, get a hold of them, and keep them nearby.

6. Now you are ready to start translating. Preferably, you will be using a computer. If this is too intimidating, write it out the first time. It will take longer, but you will have more time to think. Remember, your objective is to translate on computer, not longhand. These days, if you want to earn money translating, you have to submit text on disk. There are hardly any exceptions to this requirement.

7. Do a draft translation. Go over the draft. Do the best you can to make the English sound like good, clear, correct English, which does not sound like German, and does not retain any German forms in either style, format, or any technical points. Be sure you did not omit anything. Ask yourself if you succeeded in conveying the correct sense of every idea and every word in the source text. Be sure you are comfortable with every single word you chose in English, and that you have no doubts or hesitations. If, after all this, you do have some questions, do not worry. No one expects you to do perfect work the first time around. You will do better next time.

8.   Now that you have accomplished your translation, figure out the time it took you to reach your final version (including all the previous steps, namely first reading, research, draft, and final copy).

9.   Make a list of the words, passages, and concepts in the text where you encountered difficulty, and keep for future reference. This kind of record keeping will help you improve your performance, and serve as a reminder not to repeat the same mistake twice.

10.   Print out your corrected and edited text.

1.   Turn to the English translation in Section 3, and compare it to yours. Next read the notes concerning the pitfalls and salient points of this text very carefully, and see how they compare to your own experience with the text. They may not necessarily coincide with everything you experienced personally, but they do provide you with some tips on the dos and don'ts of technical translation.

2.   The most important thing for you to keep in mind as you compare your translation to the one in Section 3, is that there is no one absolutely correct way of translating a text. Many words can be translated in more than one way. Many sentences can be structured in more than one way. Many ideas can be conveyed in different words. In fact, your translation may turn out to be just as good, and in some spots even better than the one in the book.

3.   Keep track of the shortcomings of your translation. The areas you are interested in are the following:

Omissions - did you fail to translate any particular word or phrase, or even paragraph?

Format - does your format follow the original (breaking into paragraphs, for instance)?

Mistranslations - did you mistranslate any particular word?

Unknown words - were there any words you were not able to translate?

Meaning - did you miss the meaning of any particular phrase or sentence?

Spelling - did you misspell a word?

Grammar - did you make any grammatical mistakes?

Punctuation - did you mispunctuate or miss any punctuation marks?

Clarity - did you fail to clearly convey the meaning of any particular part of the text?

Consistency - did you call something by one name, and then by another without good reason?

Cognates - were you "tripped" by a word in the source text, whereby you mistranslated it because it looked the same, though it changes meaning in the target language (for instance, the word "actual"("*aktuell*") exists in both English and German, but means two different things)?

Style - are you satisfied with the way your translation reflects the style of the original (for example, the original is written in a clear, direct style, while the translation sounds more complex and indirect)?

These are some of the questions you have to ask yourself. As you go on to translate other texts, always keep these questions in mind as you self-assess your translation. By improving your performance in the above areas, you are on your way to becoming an accomplished translator.

Part One

Translation : German into English

Zweibeiner auf den Bäumen

5 **Der Mensch lernte den aufrechten Gang nicht erst in der Savanne**

Sie waren nicht nur eine der berühmtesten Bands der Rockgeschichte. Die Beatles hinterließen auch in der Anthropologie ihre Spuren. Als Donald Johanson und Tim White in Hadar, Äthiopien, 1974 das Skelett eines weiblichen Urmenschen untersuchten, dröhnte der Beatles-
10 Song "Lucy in the Sky with Diamonds" durchs Lager. Den Ohrwurm im Kopf, nannten die Wissenschaftler das Fossil Lucy.

Sie wurde eine Berühmtheit - nicht nur ihres griffigen Namens wegen. Rund 3,1 Millionen Jahre alt, bildete sie lange das älteste Zeugnis in der Evolutionsgeschichte des Menschen. Und sie galt
15 als Stellvertreterin jener Art, die den aufrechten Gang erfand und auf zwei Beinen die Savannen Afrikas eroberte.

Das hat sich nun geändert. In der neuesten Ausgabe des Wissenschaftsmagazins "Nature" berichtet eine Forschergruppe um die kenianische Anthropologin Meave Leakey von
20 Fossilfunden aus der Frühzeit des Menschen, die die Kenntnisse der Wissenschaftler zur Entstehung des aufrechten Gangs revolutionieren.

Die versteinerten, 4,1 Millionen Jahre alten Knochen einer bislang unbekannten Urmenschenart belegen, daß der Mensch bereits gut eine halbe Million Jahre früher auf zwei Beinen ging.
25 Bislang galten die etwa 3,7 Millionen Jahre alten, versteinerten Fußspuren von Laetoli (Tansania) - entdeckt von Meaves Schwiegermutter Mary - als die ältesten Zeugnisse des aufrechten Gangs.

Noch viel bedeutender aber: Die neuen Funde beweisen zusammen mit anderen, daß der Affe die zweibeinige Lebensweise nicht etwa lernte, um im hohen Gras der Savannen den Überblick
30 zu bewahren. Statt dessen erfand die Evolution den aufrechten Gang zu einer Zeit, als unsere Ahnen noch in den Bäumen kletterten.

Leakey und ihre Kollegen tauften den frühen Zweibeiner - mit einem Körpergewicht von 46 bis 55 Kilogramm war er etwa so groß wie ein Schimpanse - auf den Namen "Australopithecus
35 anamensis". (Übersetzt bedeutet das der "Südaffe vom See".)

Doch der Name ist allenfalls zur Hälfte zutreffend. Nur der Kopf des neuen Urmenschen war noch affenähnlich, mit dem typischen fliehenden Kinn. Die fossilen Reste des Fortbewegungsapparats unter den 21 Fundstücken aus Kanapoi und Allia Bay am Rudolfsee in
40 Kenia tragen indes erstaunlich fortschrittliche - sprich menschenähnliche - Züge.

So fand sich ein versteinertes Schienbein, das an seinem dem Knie zugewandten Teil Ausformungen aufweist, die für den modernen Menschen typisch sind: Sie erlauben das Strecken des Beins. Am unteren Endstück zeigen sich Spezialisierungen der Sehnen und Muskelansätze, die auf eine senkrechte Stellung des Fußes zu den Beinen hinweisen.

5

Die Entwicklung des aufrechten Gangs setzte also bereits früh in der Geschichte des Menschen ein - stagnierte aber bald. Untersuchungen von Ronald Clarke und Phillip Tobias aus Südafrika zeigen, daß die Füße auch vor 3,5 Millionen Jahren noch nicht ausschließlich an das Bodenleben angepaßt waren. Aufgrund der Analyse schon länger bekannter fossiler Fußknochen aus der

10 Höhle von Sterkfontein nahe Johannesburg entdeckten sie, daß der große Zeh den anderen vier nicht mehr gegenüberstand. Andererseits hatte er seine parallele Lage - wie beim modernen Menschen - noch nicht erreicht. Diese Zwischenform ermöglichte den Vormenschen neben dem Greifen und Klettern auch die Fortbewegung auf dem Boden.

15 "Eine Lebensweise, die auch heute noch der Gorilla pflegt", erläutert Peter Andrews vom Londoner Natural History Museum. Der Anthropologe geht davon aus, daß die Urmenschen durchaus befähigt waren, auf zwei Beinen am Boden nach Nahrung zu suchen. Sie verbrachten jedoch noch sehr viel Zeit in den Bäumen.

20 Keinesfalls also lernten die Urmenschen den aufrechten Gang in den Savannen Afrikas. Statt dessen wurde er im Wald erfunden und brachte so viele Vorteile mit sich, daß sich die Hominiden schon früh in mehrere Arten aufspalteten. Diese besiedelten verschiedenste Lebensräume zwischen Wald und Savanne. Die Folge erläutert Meave Leakey: "Der Stammbaum der Vormenschen im Pliozän, vor drei bis fünf Millionen Jahren, glich mehr einem

25 Busch als einem Stamm."

Erst kürzlich beschrieb der Anthropologe Tim White von der Universität von Kalifornien einen dieser neuen Urmenschen. Mit einem Alter von 4,4 Millionen Jahren nimmt der "Ardipithecus ramidus" nun Lucys Platz als ältestes Fossil der Evolution des Menschen ein. Unter den

30 Überbleibseln der Art, die noch auf den Bäumen lebte, befinden sich, so erzählen die Anthropologen, auch versteinerte Knochen von Extremitäten, die auf Zweibeinigkeit verweisen.

Im weiteren Verlauf der Evolution starben die ersten Zweibeiner alle aus. Welcher das Erfolgsmodell war, das zum weisen Homo sapiens wurde, ist unbekannt.

35

Lohengrin: Das erste Blind-Date

Romantische Oper in 3 Akten über ein Rendezvous mit einem Unbekannten

5   Die Oper der Opern: romantisch überschwenglich, melodienselig und wahrlich der Wunder voll. Da kommt der rettende Ritter in höchster Not, von einem Schwan transportiert. Da soll die Gerettete ihren Helden zwar lieben, aber nie nach Namen und Herkunft fragen. Unter Dankestränen verspricht sie alles. Will dann natürlich doch wissen, wer ihr Strahlemann sei. Stirbt am Ende. Und Lohengrin muß enttäuscht zum Heiligen Gral zurück. Seine Hoffnungen
10 auf die Wonnen der irdischen Liebe und das absolute Vertrauen eines Weibes waren zu groß gewesen. Wie der "Lohengrin" entstand und was er bedeutet.

Auf der Höhe seiner Kunst und seines Instrumentieren-Könnens, befeuert von den triumphalen Erfahrungen, die er mit den vorangegangenen Werken ("Rienzi", 1842; "Fliegender Holländer",
15 1843; "Tannhäuser", 1845) gemacht hatte, so dichtete und komponierte Wagner, mittlerweile gefeierter sächsischer Hofkapellmeister, 1846/47 den "Lohengrin". Er war damals noch keine 35 Jahre alt! Danach überstürzten sich die Ereignisse. Naiv, aber enthusiastisch beteiligte sich Wagner aktiv an der Revolution von 1848. Mußte emigrieren. Im Züricher Exil, zwischen 1848 und 1853, komponierte er dann kaum. Entwickelte vielmehr theoretisch seine neuen Ideen des
20 "Musikdramas", wie er sie dann vor allem im "Ring des Nibelungen" und im "Tristan" verwirklichte.

Der "Lohengrin" war also ein schwungvoll-pathetischer, melodiöser Abschied vom Hergebrachten. Romantisch-verklärtes, feierlich-wunderliches reizt stets auch zum Spott. "Wann geht
25 der nächste Schwan?" Nestroy verfaßte sogar eine von Herzen gehässige Parodie, in der Lohengrin von einem Schaf apportiert wird: "Nun sei bedankt, mein gutes Schaf/Kehr' wieder heim zum Zauberschlaf".

Alles das hat dem "Lohengrin" nichts anhaben können. Noch zu Lebzeiten des Komponisten
30 wurde er in 80 Städten der ganzen Welt aufgeführt! In Berlin, London, Moskau, Melbourne - - aber auch in Kleinstädten wie Görlitz, Gotha, Nizza. Bereits das Vorspiel zum 1. Akt ist ein (von Thomas Mann heiß geliebtes) Instrumentationswunder. Die flimmernden Geigen symbolisieren, daß etwas Heiliges sich aus reiner Höhe in die irdische Wirklichkeit senkt. Dem korrespondiert das düstere Vorspiel zum 2. Akt. Ein leises, depressives Nachtstück. Und dann
35 die feurig brillante, reißerisch auftrumpfende Ouvertüre zum Schlußakt eine allzu vorbehaltlos jubilierende Hochzeitsmusik.

Zu Beginn wartet Elsa von Brabant, des Brudermords angeklagt, passiv entrückt auf einen erträumten, helfenden Wunderritter. Das Wunder geschieht: Lohengrins Schwanen-Auftritt.
40 Herrisch äußert der Held sein Frageverbot. Dann besiegt der Schwanen-Ritter den verleumderischen Telramund. Alles gut?

Im 2. Akt agieren die besiegten Bösen. Telramunds schlimme Gattin, die politisierende Heidin Ortrud (eine Bombenrolle) provoziert Elsa zu tiefen Zweifeln. Kann alles mit rechten Dingen
45 zugegangen sein, wenn ein wilder Schwan einen vorsichtshalber namenlosen Ritter anschleppte? Ein nachdenkliches Ensemble, Richard Strauß bewunderte es, beschließt grandios die Szene.

Im Schlußakt vermag Lohengrins glühende Liebe Elsas Zweifel keineswegs zu beruhigen. "Es kann von schlimmsten Folgen sein, wenn man nicht zur rechten Zeit zu Bett geht!" spöttelte Nietzsche schadenfroh. In einem Riesenduett fragt Elsa. Wäre Lohengrin ein unnahbarer Gott, hätte sie sich gewiß zurückgehalten. Aber da sie einen zärtlichen Mann liebt, möchte Frau schon wissen, wer er ist. Auch wenn es das Leben kostet.

5

word count: 1169

ASSIGNMENT 2: LEGAL

1 Einführung

5 **1.1 Anlaß**

Nach Punkt III.8 der Verwaltungsvorschrift zur Konkretisierung der auf die Deutsche Bundespost TELEKOM weiterübertragenen Befugnis zur Ausübung des Netzmonopols des Bundes vom 19.09.91 (im folgenden "Verwaltungsvorschrift Netzmonopol" genannt) und nach Punkt IX.8 der
10 Verwaltungsvorschrift zur Konkretisierung der auf die Deutsche Bundespost TELEKOM weiterübertragenen Befugnis Ausübung des Telefondienstmonopols des Bundes vom 13.07.92 (im folgenden "Verwaltungsvorschrift Telefondienstmonopol" genannt)

"dürfen die im Monopolbereich anfallenden Kundeninformationen von der Deutschen
15 *Bundespost TELEKOM für Leistungen auf den Wettbewerbsmärkten nur insoweit verwendet werden, wie diese auch den Wettbewerbern zur Verfügung gestellt werden. Die entsprechenden datenschutzrechtlichen Vorschriften bleiben unberührt."*

1.2 Auftrag
20
Die daraus resultierenden Aufträge an die Deutsche Bundespost TELEKOM lauten:

  •entsprechend Punkt IX.8 Verwaltungsvorschrift Telefondienstmonopol

25 *"Die Deutsche Bundespost TELEKOM ist verpflichtet, dem Bundesminister für Post und Telekommunikation unverzüglich eine Konzeption vorzulegen, aus der hervorgeht, auf welche Art und Weise eine mißbräuchliche Verwendung von im Monopolbereich anfallenden Kundeninformationen verhindert wird. Sofern bis zu diesem Zeitpunkt keine Konzeption vorgelegt wird, oder die Konzeption nicht den notwendigen Anforderungen genügt, behält sich*
30 *der Bundesminister für Post und Telekommunikation vor, eine weitere Konzeption abzufordern."*

  •entsprechend Punkt III.8 Verwaltungsvorschrift Netzmonopol

35 *"Die Deutsche Bundespost TELEKOM ist verpflichtet, dem Bundesminister für Post und Telekommunikation bis spätestens zum 30.Juni 1992 eine Konzeption vorzulegen, aus der hervorgeht, auf welche Art und Weise eine mißbräuchliche Verwendung von im Monopol-bereich anfallenden Kundeninformationen verhindert wird."*

40 Entsprechend obiger Verwaltungsvorschriften ist es Ziel dieser Aufträge, auch in diesem Bezugsbereich "Chancengleichheit zwischen der Deutschen Bundespost TELEKOM als Wettbewerber und privaten Nutzern herzustellen".

1.3 Position der TELEKOM

☐ TELEKOM fühlt sich dem Grundsatz eines fairen Wettbewerbs im Umgang mit Monopolleistungen und im Sinne des Wettbewerbsrechts verpflichtet.

☐ TELEKOM ist entschlossen, einen diskriminierungsfreien Umgang mit den im Monopolbereich anfallenden Kundeninformationen zu gewährleisten.

1.4 Ausgangslage

Entsprechend der Aufgabenstellung aus dem § 1 PostVerfG obliegen der Deutschen Bundespost TELEKOM Wahrnehmung ihres öffentlichen Auftrags, Infrastrukturdienste (Monopol- und Pflichtleistungen) bereitzustellen und die notwendige Infrastruktur zu sichern, im nationalen und internationalen Bereich unternehmerische und betriebliche Aufgaben des Fernmeldewesens.[sic] Monopol- und Wettbewerbsleistungen werden von der Deutschen Bundespost TELEKOM gemeinsam erbracht.

Daraus ergibt sich für TELEKOM die Möglichkeit von ökonomisch sinnvollen Verbundnutzungen unter Berücksichtigung der in § 37 Abs.4 PostVerfG (Quersubventionierung) festgelegten Grundsätze.

1.5 Bisherige Entwicklung

Unmittelbar nach dem Erlaß der Verwaltungsvorschriften Netz- und Telefondienstmonopol begann TELEKOM mit den notwendigen Untersuchungen im Sinne des vorstehenden Auftrages. Hierbei zeigte es sich schon bald, daß der Begriff "Kundeninformation" nicht ausreichte, um die in diesem Bereich entstehenden Probleme zu beschreiben und die Verpflichtung von TELEKOM zur Chancengleichheit zu erfüllen. Einvernehmlich mit dem BMPT wurde deshalb der Begriff "Kundeninformation" durch den besser geeigneten Begriff "Monopolinformationen" ersetzt.

1.5.1 Organisatorische Folgen aus den Verwaltungsvorschriften

1.) In der Generaldirektion TELEKOM wurde ein Fachbereich u.a. mit den Aufgaben "Wettbewerbsneutralität und Chancengleichheit in den Monopolbereichen" eingerichtet. Dieser Fachbereich ist dem Vorstand unmittelbar berichtspflichtig. Die Aufgaben dieses Fachbereiches wurden aus gegebenem Anlaß um den Auftrag "Ansprechpartner für Fragen zum diskriminierungsfreien Umgang der TELEKOM mit Monopolleistungen" erweitert.

2.) Bei den Fernmeldeämtern wurde eine den Monopolbereichen zugeordnete unabhängige Dienststelle eingerichtet, in der die "diskriminierungsfreie Bereitstellung von anschluß- und übertragungswegbezogenen Daten" sowie eine entsprechende Bestandsdatenführung bei Monopolübertragungswegen zu den wichtigsten wettbewerbsneutral wahrzunehmenden Aufgaben zählt.

Da diese Dienststelle zur Wettbewerbsneutralität verpflichtet ist, wurde sie in dieser Funktion der Generaldirektion TELEKOM unmittelbar unterstellt; die Dienststellenleiter sind für Wettbewerber ebenfalls unmittelbare Ansprechpartner bei vermeintlichen Abweichungen von TELEKOM von den Grundsätzen zur Chancengleichheit.

3.) TELEKOM hat erklärt, das im Rahmen des Projekts "TELEKOM Kontakt" bei der Neuorganisation der Fernmeldeämter die erforderliche Wettbewerbsneutralität durch entsprechende organisatorische Änderungen in der Außenorganisation sichergestellt sein wird.

1.5.2 Diskriminierungsfreier Umgang mit Monopolinformationen

In diesem Zusammenhang nimmt die vorstehend genannte Dienststelle insbesondere folgende Aufgaben wahr:

Kundenkontakte, Kundenanschreiben, neutrale Kundenberatung im Monopolbereich, Bereitstellung von Monopolinformationen, diskriminierungsfreier Monopoldatentransfer zu den BMPT-Außenstellen, diskriminierungsfreie Maßnahmen bei Verstoß gegen die EU-Bestimmungen, wenn TK-Anlagen nicht den grundlegenden Anforderungen der EU entsprechen, wettbewerbsneutrale Behandlung von Kundenaufträgen, wenn Wettbewerber ein berechtigtes Interesse an der vertraulichen Behandlung von Informationen über ihre eigenen Kunden haben, sowie chanchengleiche Hinweise auf Produkte der Wettbewerbsbereiche aus Anlaß von Maßnahmen in Monopolbereichen (z.B. bei Einschaltung von Vermittlungsstellen).

1.5.3 Bereitstellung von Monopolinformationen zur Verbesserung der Chancengleicheit der Wettbewerber

Zu diesem Zweck können von TELEKOM bereits Daten der Telefonkunden ("Telefonbuchdaten") und Verzonungsdaten erworben werden; die Bereitstellung von Längendaten bei Monopolübertragungswegen ist in Vorbereitung. Einschalttermine von digitalen Ortsvermittlungsstellen können im Btx-Dienst abgerufen werden.

Als der Öffentlichkeit zugänglich gemachte Monopolinformationen mit weitreichender volkswirtschaftlicher Bedeutung ist in diesem Zusammenhang auch die Konzeption der Deutschen Bundespost TELEKOM zur Realisierung eines offenen Netzzugangs zu den Funktionen des Telefonnetzes zu sehen.

Die bisher veranlaßten Maßnahmen sind Grundlage der Konzeption und werden folglich innerhalb der Konzeption weiterentwickelt werden und wurden - z.T. unabhängig vom Inhalt der Verwaltungsvorschriften - bereits unmittelbar nach der Postreform I in Übereinstimmung mit dem BMPT entwickelt und den einschlägigen Fachverbänden der Wettbewerber vorgestellt.

word count: 770

Einleitung

5   Ziel des Chemikaliengesetzes ist es, Mensch und Umwelt vor gefährlichen Chemikalien zu schützen. Bei Inkrafttreten des Chemikaliengesetzes im Jahre 1982 wurden die zur Erkennung des toxischen Potentials eines Stoffes für erforderlich gehaltenen Prüfungen zusammengestellt und detaillierte allgemeine Prüfvorschriften ausgearbeitet, die seither mehrfach präzisiert bzw. verbessert worden sind.

10

Die Erfahrungen, die der Fachbereich Chemikalienbewertung in den 12 Jahren seit Inkrafttreten des Chemikaliengesetzes sammeln konnte, haben zur Ausarbeitung von Vorschlägen für substanzspezifische Teststrategien zur gezielteren und Versuchstiere einsparenden toxikologischen Bewertung neuer Chemikalien der Grundstufe des Chemikaliengesetzes geführt,

15   die im Tätigkeitsbericht des Bundesgesundheitsamtes 1991 veröffentlicht worden sind [1]. Sie bilden eine der Grundlagen für die Ausarbeitung von neuen Prüfstrategien durch die Arbeitsgruppe "Fortentwicklung toxikologischer Prüfmethoden im Rahmen des Chemikaliengetzes".

20   Im folgenden werden die Ergebnisse der Auswertung der Unterlagen zu neuen Chemikalien nach dem Chemikaliengesetz in bezug auf die Bestimmung der akuten Toxizität und die auf dieser Basis erarbeiteten speziellen Vorschläge für eine tiersparende Vorgehensweise zur Ermittlung der akuten dermalen Toxizität vorgestellt.

25   **Auswertung der Meldeunterlagen für Chemikalien mit einer Reinheit >95%**

Im Rahmen der Meldeverfahren nach dem Chemikaliengesetz sind bis Mitte des Jahres 1993 EU-weit in mehr als 1000 Meldeverfahren über 1000 verschiedene chemische Stoffe angemeldet worden. Im August 1993 waren insgesamt 1012 unterschiedliche Chemikalien gemeldet:

30

-    532 Stoffe sind als Reinchemikalien anzusehen, weil sie weniger als 5% Verunreinigungen enthalten und diese Verunreinigungen für die hier betrachteten toxischen Eigenschaften ohne Relevanz sind.

35   -   480 Stoffe stellen Mischungen von unterschiedlichen chemischen Substanzen dar.

Da das Chemikaliengesetz für neue Chemikalien detaillierte physikalisch-chemische und toxikologische Prüfunterlagen zur Bestimmung physikalisch-chemischer Stoffeigenschaften und toxischer Stoffwirkungen mit Hilfe standardisierter Prüfmethoden vorschreibt, liegen der

40   Abteilung Chemikalienbewertung zu allen EU-weit angemeldeten Neustoffen vollständige und während des Meldeverfahrens von den Behörden überprüfte Stoffdatensätze vor, die direkt miteinander verglichen werden können.

Um Zusammenhänge zwischen den physikalisch-chemischen Stoffeigenschaften einerseits und akut toxischen, lokal reizenden und hautsensibilisierenden Stoffwirkungen andererseits aufzufinden, wurden die Prüfunterlagen von 345 Reinchemikalien exemplarisch ausgewertet. Ziel ist die Ausarbeitung EDV-gestützter Struktur-Wirkungs-Modelle (SAR-Modelle) zur Vorhersage akut toxischer, lokal reizender und hautsensibilisierender Stoffwirkungen [2].

Von den 345 untersuchten Chemikalien sind insgesamt 163 (47,2 %) als akut toxisch, lokal reizend bzw. hautsensibilisierend eingestuft und mit entsprechenden Gefahrenhinweisen (R-Sätzen) gekennzeichnet:

- 80 Stoffe (23,2 %) als lokal reizend oder ätzend am Auge,
- 74 Stoffe (21,5 %) als hautsensibilisierend,
- 65 Stoffe (18,8 %) als oral mindergiftig oder giftig,
- 55 Stoffe (15,9 %) als lokal reizend oder ätzend an der Haut,
- 8 Stoffe (2,3 %) als dermal mindergiftig oder giftig.

Eine genauere Analyse der kennzeichnungspflichtigen akut toxischen und lokal reizenden Wirkungen der untersuchten Stoffe hat folgende Ergebnisse erbracht[3]:

- Orale Verabreichung ätzender Stoffe führt zwar sehr häufig, aber keineswegs immer zum Tod der Versuchstiere: Von den aufgefundenen 20 ätzenden Stoffen haben fünf eine orale LD50 >2000mg/kg.
- Dermale Applikation wirkt nur in sehr seltenen Fällen akut toxisch.
- Die untersuchten dermal akut toxischen Stoffe sind in keinem Fall ausschließlich wegen dieser einen toxischen Wirkung zu kennzeichnen, sondern alle acht dermal akut toxischen Stoffe wirken auch oral akut toxisch und zeigen zusätzlich lokale Ätzwirkungen mit deutlich ausgeprägten klinischen Vergiftungssymptomen (Tab. 1, Stoffe 1-8). Von den Stoffen aber, die weder als oral toxisch noch als lokal reizend bewertet wurden, hat kein Stoff eine einstufungsrelevante akute dermale Toxizität gezeigt.
- Durchaus nicht alle stark hautreizenden Stoffe wirken auch stark augenreizend.
- Viele Stoffe erzeugen zwar ernste Augenschäden, reizen die Haut aber nicht oder nur unwesentlich.

Vorhersagbarkeit der akuten dermalen Toxizität

Die bisherige Auswertung der Prüfunterlagen nach dem Chemikaliengesetz hat gezeigt, daß es möglich sein sollte vorherzusagen, ob die Applikation eines chemischen Stoffes auf die Haut von Versuchstieren innerhalb von 14 Tagen zum Tod der Tiere führen könnte. Aus der Zusammenschau bestimmter physikalisch-chemischer Stoffdaten [4-8] und den Beobachtungen bei den Prüfungen auf akute orale Toxizität und auf lokale Reizwirkungen an Haut und Augen sollte sich erkennen lassen, ob ein Stoff in so relevanter Menge die Haut penetrieren kann, daß akut deutliche klinische Symptome bzw. eine einstufungsrelevante LD50 zu erwarten sind. Tierversuche zur Bestimmung der akuten dermalen LD50 wären dann nur noch für die sehr wenigen Chemikalien erforderlich, deren akute dermale Toxizität sich nicht mit der erforderlichen Sicherheit theoretisch vorhersagen läßt.

Aus Tabelle 1 (Stoffe 1-8) ist zu ersehen, daß alle aufgefundenen dermal akut toxischen Stoffe nicht nur dermal, sondern zusätzlich auch oral akut toxisch wirken. Außerdem ätzen sie alle die Haut und/oder die Augen und erzeugen dabei neben den Ätzwirkungen auch deutlich erkennbar Vergiftungserscheinungen (in Draize-Tests wurden entsprechende systemische Wirkungen
5 beobachtet).

Des weiteren ist zu erkennen, daß diese Chemikalien relativ gut wasserlöslich sind, denn aus den Auswertungen geht hervor, daß im Zusammenhang mit akut toxischen Stoffwirkungen erst eine Löslichkeit <0,1 c/l als "schlecht wasserlöslich" zu betrachten ist. Sieben der acht Stoffe sind
10 auch relativ gut in Fett löslich (als "schlechte Fettlöslichkeit" werden in Zusammenhang mit akut toxischen Wirkungen Löslichkeiten <0,1 g/kg bewertet).

Der Stoff Nr.4 ist in vielen Beziehungen bemerkenswert; er ist zwar schlecht fettlöslich und wirkt daher auch nicht hautreizend [3]. Er weist aber eine ungewöhnlich niedrige orale LD50
15 von 150 mg/kg auf (weshalb er als "oral giftig" zu kennzeichnen ist), und er ätzt nicht nur die Augen - im Augenreiztest sind zwei der drei Versuchstiere innerhalb von 48 Stunden gestorben.

word count: 812

Ein erster Schritt vorwärts in Guatemala

Im Januar 1992 vereinbarte die Empresa Eléctrica de Guatemala S.A. (EEGSA) - der wichtigste Energienetzbetreiber in Guatemala - einen fünfzehnjährigen Abnabmevertrag mit einer lokalen Kraftwerksgesellschaft. Fast unmittelbar danach verkaufte die Gesellschaft diese Projektrechte an die Enron Power Development Corporation, dem Tochterunternehmen einer großen US-ame-rikanischen Erdgasgesellschaft mit Beteiligungen an verschiedenen unabhängigen Energieprojekten. Das Projekt besteht aus zwanzig 5,5-Megawatt-Generatoren, die auf einem Lastkahn in Puerto Quetzal in Stellung gebracht sind, der als Kraftwerk für die Grundversorgung fungiert. Mit dem Projekt vergrößert sich die Erzeugungskapazität Guatemalas um 12 Prozent, und seine effektive Kapazität um etwa 15 Prozent.

Die Preise in der Energieabnahmevereinbarung sind in US-Dollar ausgedrückt. Aufgrund der Vereinbarung muß die EEGSA der Projektgesellschaft, der Puerto Quetzal Power Corporation (PQP), wöchentlich festgelegte Zahlungen für die Bereitstellung der Kapazität leisten, vorausgesetzt, daß die PQP Mindestnormen hinsichtlich der Verfügbarkeit erfüllt. Darüber hinaus hat die EEGSA wöchentliche Zahlungen für die Energie zu leisten, wobei die Abnahme von mindestens 50 Prozent der Energieerzeugung garantiert wird, und die EEGSA bietet zusätzliche Unterstützung hinsichtlich der Stellung von Sicherheiten und Dokumentation, um ihre Verpflichtungen gegenüber der PQP zu untermauern. Die EEGSA hat die Wahl, die PQP in US-Dollar zu bezahlen oder in Quetzals (auf Grundlage des aktuellen Wechselkurses). Für den Fall eines Abfalls der Energieleistung auf unter 50 Prozent zahlt die PQP der EEGSA eine Strafgebühr. Entsprechend der Vereinbarung muß das Projekt die Energie zu wettbewerbsfähigen Preisen liefern. Unter den gegenwärtigen Annahmen über die Kapazitätsausnutzung, die eine Leistungsverschlechterung im Zeitablauf unterstellen, bezahlt die EEGSA durchschnittlich 0,07 Dollar je Kilowattstunde während der gesamten Laufzeit des Projekts; dies entspricht in etwa den langfristigen Grenzkosten für den Großteil der Energieversorgung in Guatemala.

Die PQP hat einen Teil der Risiken dadurch eliminiert, daß sie Verträge über die schlüsselfertige Herstellung, den Betrieb und die Wartung sowie die Brennstofflieferung abschloß. Das Kraftwerk nahm den Betrieb Ende Februar 1993 auf, und zwar termingerecht und ohne Kostenüberschreitung. Eine Überprüfung des Betriebs in der Anfangszeit deutet darauf hin, daß die PQP einen hohen Nutzungsgrad der vorhandenen Kapazität erreicht hat, die Einnahmen und der Nettogewinn mit den Prognosen übereinstimmen und die Konversion von Quetzals in US-Dollar kein Problem darstellte. Nach der Beobachtung der Erfahrungen der EEGSA mit der PQP hat das Instituto Nacional de Electrificación - ein staatseigenes Unternehmen, das für die Energieerzeugung, die Übertragung und die Verteilung auf die Haushalte außerhalb von

Guatemala-Stadt verantwortlich ist - damit begonnen, andere Energieabnahmevereinbarungen mit unabhängigen Erzeugern auszuhandeln.

Die gebührenpflichtigen Straßen Mexikos: Ein starker Anstoß, der ins Stocken geriet

Unter Infrastrukturprojekten stellt man sich oft Objekte vor, die hohe Baukosten verursachen und nur begrenzt produktiven Nutzen spenden. Dies kann unter privater wie öffentlicher Regie gleichermaßen der Fall sein, wenn nicht die richtige Anreizstruktur angewendet wird.

In Vorbereitung auf ein ehrgeiziges Straßenbauprogramm mit einer Länge von 6.000 Kilometer stellte eine mexikanische Regierungsbehörde hastige Verkehrs- und Kostenprognosen auf und bereitete die Straßenkonzeption vor. Die Qualität dieser Schätzungen und Konzepte reichte bei weitem nicht an die Standards heran, die für solche Projekte erforderlich sind. Gleichzeitig war die Kreditvergabe der staatseigenen Banken an die Projektbetriebe zur Errichtung gebührenpflichtiger Straßen nicht mit der üblichen Projektüberprüfung und -bewertung verbunden.

Zwar wurden die Konzessionen für den Bau und Betrieb der Straßen aufgrund verschiedener Kriterien vergeben; die Investoren, die zusagten, die Straßen innerhalb kürzester Zeit an den Staat rückzuübertragen, wurden jedoch besonders bevorzugt. Kurzfristige Konzessionen wurden zum Teil deshalb begünstigt, weil die Sorge bestand, daß nur kurzfristige Finanzmittel zur Verfügung stehen würden. Der Versuch, Erfolge innerhalb der Legislaturperiode der neuen Regierung zu erzielen, schuf ebenfalls das Gefühl besonderer Dringlichkeit. Auf der anderen Seite handelten die Anleger Gebührensätze heraus, die eine Rendite innerhalb der Konzessionsperiode versprachen. Die Gebühren waren daher in aller Regel fünf- bis zehnmal höher als für vergleichbare Strecken in den Vereinigten Staaten.

Bei derartig hohen Gebühren stellte sich nicht das Verkehrsaufkommen ein - den alten, gebührenfreien Straßen wurde der Vorzug gegeben, obwohl die Reisezeit üblicherweise doppelt so lang war. Darüber hinaus lagen die Kostenüberschreitungen im Durchschnitt bei über 50 Prozent der projektierten Kosten. (Der Highway of the Sun von Cuernavaca nach Acapulco kostete zum Beispiel 2,1 Mrd Dollar und damit mehr als das Doppelte als ursprünglich geschätzt.)

Um die Lage zu verbessern, hat die mexikanische Regierung verschiedene Schritte ergriffen. In vielen Fällen wurden die Konzessionsperioden von zehn oder fünfzehn Jahren auf dreißig Jahre verlängert. Wo Gemeinschaftsunternehmen größere Aussichten auf finanzielle Tragfähigkeit boten, wurden Abschnitte der gebührenpflichtigen Straße unter einheitlicher Leitung zusammengefaßt. Schwereren Fahrzeugen kann der Zugang zum alten Straßennetz verwehrt werden, da Gewichtsbegrenzungen auferlegt und durchgesetzt werden.

Es gibt Anzeichen dafür, daß die schwierigste Periode vorüber ist. Auf lange Sicht sollten die Zusammenlegung gebührenpflichtiger Straßen, längere Konzessionszeiträume und realistischere Verkehrs- und Kostenprojektionen, im Verein mit wirtschaftlichem Wachstum und größerer finanzieller Verantwortung auf seiten der Privatbetreiber der Projekte, beträchtliche Renditen für diese Infrastrukturinvestitionen erbringen.

Multiplikation der Mittel durch Bürgschaften in Thailand

5 Zur Anregung der privaten Kreditvergabe entwickelt die thailändische Regierung die Thai-Bürgschafts-Fazilität; diese sichert Darlehen ab, die private Finanzinstitute an kommunale und private Betreiber von städtischer Umwelt-Infrastruktur vergeben. Die Fazilität soll als Gesellschaft mit öffentlicher und privater Beteiligung errichtet werden und unter privater Leitung stehen. Das angestrebte Datum für die Aufnahme der Tätigkeit der Einrichtung ist der Juni

10 1994.

Aufgrund mangelnder Erfahrungen mit der Kreditvergabe an Kommunen, sind diese in den Augen der Kreditinstitute Schuldner mit hohem Risiko. Angesichts der Annahme hoher Projektrisiken sind die Kreditgeber zurückhaltend bei der Vergabe von Darlehen mit einer

15 Laufzeit von mehr als acht Jahren; dieser Zeitraum ist zu kurz, um die Investitionen in die Umwelt-Infrastruktur zu amortisieren.

Indem die staatliche Kreditsicherungsstelle zugunsten privater Betreiber und Kommunen Bürgschaften abgibt und ihnen damit zu Darlehen von kommerziellen Geldgebern verhilft schafft

20 sie langfristige Kreditfinanzierungen. Mit zunehmender Kreditvergabe an die Kommunen wird es bald möglich sein, die Kreditwürdigkeit von Städten einzustufen und ihnen den Weg zu bahnen, Anleihen zu begeben. Zehn Provinzstädte, die fünf Städte der Großregion von Bangkok und Bangkok selbst dürften aller Erwartung nach die Hauptnutznießer von Darlehensbürgschaften für Investitionen in die Abwasseraufbereitung, die Abfuhr und Beseitigung von Müll und die

25 Versorgung mit Trinkwasser sein.

Für die ersten beiden Betriebsjahre wird erwartet, daß die Bürgschafts-Fazilität 75 Mio Dollar erhält. Die Kreditvergabe wird fünf- bis achtmal so hoch sein wie these Garantiemittel. Über einen Zeitraum von fünf Jahren soll die Einrichtung den Projektionen zufolge mit Mitteln von

30 150 Mio Dollar ausgestattet sein und ein Darlehensvolumen von bis zu 1,2 Mrd Dollar für städtische Umwelt-Infrastrukturprojekte mobilisieren. Ihre Mittel bezieht sie vorwiegend von der thailändischen Regierung und durch Gelder, die sie teilweise beim USAID Housing Guaranty Program und teilweise bei thailändischen Finanzinstituten aufnimmt.

35 Um die Leistungsfähigkeit dieser Einrichtung zu gewährleisten, wurde auch ein staatliches Maßnahmenpaket geschnürt; hierzu gehören der Schwenk zum "Verursacherprinzip" bei der Umweltverschmutzung, Veränderungen in den Verwaltungsverfahren und eine größere Dezentralisierung im Entscheidungsprozeß.

40 *word count: 1106*

Bipeds in Trees

The Savanna Is Not Where Man First Learned to Walk Upright

They were not just one of the most famous bands in the history of Rock. The Beatles also left their mark in anthropology. The Beatles' song "Lucy in the Sky with Diamonds" reverberated through the camp as Donald Johanson and Tim White studied the skeleton of a primeval female in Hadar, Ethiopia in 1974. With the tune lingering in their heads, the scientists dubbed the fossil "Lucy."

She became a celebrity - not just because of her catchy name. Around 3.1 million years old, she was for a long time the oldest piece of evidence in man's history of evolution. And she was considered a representative of the species that invented the upright walk and conquered the savannas of Africa on two legs.

All that is now changed. In the latest edition of the science magazine *Nature*, a team of researchers working with Kenyan anthropologist Meave Leakey, reports on fossil finds from man's early times that revolutionize scientists' knowledge about the origin of the upright walk.

The petrified 4.1-million-year-old bones of a hitherto unknown species of primeval man prove that man was walking on two legs a good half-million years earlier. Until now, the approximately 3.7-million-year-old petrified footprints of Laetoli (Tanzania) - discovered by Meave's mother-in-law Mary - were considered to be the oldest testimony to the upright walk.

But there is one thing that is much more significant: Together with other finds, the new ones prove that the ape did not learn the two-legged way of life to preserve his good overview of the tall grass of the savannas. Instead, evolution invented the upright walk at a time when our ancestors were still climbing around in the trees.

Leakey and her colleagues christened the early biped - with a body weight of about 46 to 55 kilograms, she was about as tall as a chimpanzee - "Australopithecus anamensis." (In plain language, "the Southern Ape from the Lake.")

But the name is at best only halfway apt. Only the head of the new primeval man was still ape-like, with the typically receding chin. The fossil remnants of the locomotion apparatus among the 21 pieces found in Kanapoi and Allia Bay on Lake Rudolf in Kenya, however, bear astonishing - read anthropoid - features.

One of the finds consisted of a petrified shinbone that had bulges on the part facing toward the knee that are typical of modern man; they make it possible to extend the leg. At the lower end piece one can note specialized features of the tendons and muscular attachments that point to a perpendicular position of the foot with respect to the leg.

In other words, the development of the upright walk commenced rather early in the history of man but it soon stagnated. Investigations by Ronald Clarke and Phillip Tobias from South Africa show that the feet were not yet exclusively adapted to life on the ground even 3.5 million years ago. On the basis of an analysis of long-known fossil foot bones from the Sterkfontein Cave near Johannesburg they discovered that the big toe was no longer opposite the other four toes. On the other hand, it had not yet attained its parallel position, as in modern man. This intermediate form enabled early man to move along the ground, in addition to grasping and climbing.

"A way of life still pursued by the gorilla today," explains Peter Andrews of the London Natural History Museum. The anthropologist assumes that primeval man was certainly able to seek food on the ground while moving on two legs. But he still spent a lot of time in the trees.

In other words, primeval man under no circumstances learned to walk upright in the savannas of Africa. Instead, this way of walking was invented in the forest and yielded so many advantages that hominids rather early on split into several species. They settled the most varied environments between the forest and the savanna. Meave Leakey explains the consequence of that: "The family tree of early man during the Pliocene, 3 to 5 million years ago, resembled a bush rather than a trunk."

Recently, anthropologist Tim White, of the University of California, described one of these new primeval men. With an age of 4.4 million years, *Ardipithecus ramidus* now displaces Lucy as the oldest fossil in man's evolution. The leftovers of the species that still lived in the trees - so the anthropologists tell us - also include petrified bones of extremities that point toward two-leggedness.

All of the first bipeds died out as evolution continued. It is unknown which of them was the winning model that turned into Homo sapiens.

Lohengrin: The First Blind Date

A Romantic Opera in 3 Acts, Retelling a Rendezvous with a Stranger

The opera to end all operas: romantically effusive, abundantly melodic, and truly full of wonders. Here comes the knight to the rescue, in desperate haste, pulled by a swan. The rescued damsel-in-distress is supposed to love her hero but she must never ask his name or whence he came. Amid floods of tears of gratitude, she promises everything. But she still wants to know who her knight in shining armor is. Dies in the end. Disappointed, Lohengrin must return to the Holy Grail. His hopes for the bliss of earthly love and his spouse's absolute confidence were simply too much. Here is how "Lohengrin" came about and what it means.

At the very "height of his art and his instrumentational skill, fired by the triumphant experiences he had had with his prior works ("Rienzi," 1842; "The Flying Dutchman," 1843; "Tannhäuser," 1845) - thus Wagner, at that time the feted Saxonian court conductor, wrote and composed "Lohengrin" in 1846-1847. At that time, he was not quite 35 years old! Then events happened in rapid succession. Naively but enthusiastically, Wagner actively participated in the Revolution of 1848. He had to emigrate. He hardly composed anything during his Zurich exile between 1848 and 1853. Instead, he developed the theory of his new ideas regarding "music-drama," which he then applied, above all, to "Ring des Nibelungen" and to "Tristan."

"Lohengrin," in other words, was a briskly-pathetic melodious farewell to all that was traditional. Things romantically transfigured, things solemnly wondrous were always an invitation to mockery. "When's the next swan leaving?" Nestroy even authored a heartily hateful parody in which Lohengrin is retrieved by a sheep: "Now be thanked, my good sheep / go home to your magic sleep."

But none of that got the better of "Lohengrin." During the composer's lifetime, it was still being performed on 80 stages all over the world! Not only in Berlin, London, Moscow, Melbourne - but also in small towns, such as Görlitz, Gotha, and Nice. The overture to the first act is already a miracle of instrumentation (which Thomas Mann was most fond of). The twinkling violins symbolize the fact that something holy is descending from the pure heights to earthly reality. That is offset by the somber overture to the second act. A soft, depressing nighttime piece. And then the fiery, brilliant, thrillingly overbearing overture to the final act -an entirely too-undeservedly exultant wedding tune.

In the beginning, Elsa von Brabant, accused of murdering her brother, waits passively detached for the helping, miraculous knight of her dreams. The miracle happens: Lohengrin's scene with the swan. Commandingly, the hero utters his ban on asking any questions. Then the knight-with-the-swan defeats the slanderous Telramund. So far, so good?

The defeated evil ones go into action during the second act. Telramund's nasty spouse - the politicizing heathen Ortrud (a gem of a role) - triggers deep doubts in Elsa. Was everything really as it should have been with that wild swan dragging in a knight who, just as a precaution, is nameless? A pensive group - Richard Strauss admired it - grandiosely closes the scene.

During the final act, Lohengrin's glowing love cannot in any way assuage Elsa's doubts. "Not going to bed at the right time can have the worst consequences," mocked Nietzsche gloatingly. In the course of a gigantic duet, Elsa asks the question. If Lohengrin had been an unapproachable god, she certainly would have restrained herself. But because she loves a gentle man, the lady wants to know who he is. Even if she has to pay for it with her life.

General Notes

This assignment consists of two texts adapted from articles in the popular press. It is assumed that any translator who takes his work seriously reads current newspapers and/or periodicals in both the source and target languages, to be in touch with current trends in both languages. Both English and German have always been in as state of flux, and more so today, because of communications and mass media, they are changing almost daily. A good knowledge of German ten, twenty years ago, is not applicable today, if one hasn't kept up with the times.

The first text is taken from the field of anthropology, as treated by a journalist. It is not a scholarly text, but it does contain anthropological terms, both in German and in Latin, which need to be carefully checked for spelling and accuracy. The second text is from the field of the performing arts, specifically the opera. It is written tongue-in-cheek, and if you were to translate it for publication, you would be expected to preserve the flavor of the original by choosing words in English that reflect the German style.

In comparing your translation to the one contained in this workbook, you may want to find out not only how you did in terms of accuracy, but also in terms of providing an English version which preserves the style and the spirit of the original.

Zweibeiner auf den Bäumen

Der Mensch... (line 5) - The sentence structure of the title had to be rearranged, and there are probably several ways it could be done. Also, the capitalization of titles in English differs from German.

Rockgeschichte (line 7) - The writer mixes anthropology with rock lore. This is typical of journalistic writing, which seeks to popularize subjects which are considered "dry" or too technical. What it means for the translator, is the need to have a broad background in both "heavy" and "light" subjects, and to have a natural interest and curiosity about the world around us. Also, the use of the term "rock" in German, as in almost every other language today, is indicative of how English has invaded almost every language in today's world.

Als Donald Johanson (line 8) - A key aspect of translating German into English is the sentence structure, which varies greatly between the two languages. In a sense, translating a German sentence into English means rearranging the sentence. This "rearranging" is the key to making the English sound like English, and for the beginner it means rereading the translation to make sure the sentence is both internally well-structured and relates well to the preceding and the following sentences.

Ohrwurm im Kopf (line 10) - Here a figure of speech has to be translated into a sensible English equivalent.

griffigen (line 13) - "catchy" seems to be a good way to translate this word, but certainly not the only one.

3,1 Millionen (line 13) - Decimals in English take a period, instead of the comma in German. Is this a trivial point? If you translate a contract for Siemens, it may mean a million dollar mistake, which can put you out of business.

Meave Leakey (line 19) - Should the name read "Maeve," as the Irish name is usually spelled? Did the German writer make a mistake? If so, put [sic] after the first occurrence of the name and provide the correct spelling.

Tansania (line 25) - The English replaces the "s" with a "z." With all the new countries in today's world, geographical terms require special attention.

46 bis 55 Kilogramm (lines 33-34) - The translator kept the European term, but since the English-speaking world uses mostly pounds, there are times when one needs to covert kg to lb, and km to miles.

Pliozän (page 20, line 24) - This is an example of an anthropological term that may require a short trip to the dictionary.

Lohengrin

Blind-Date, Rendezvous (lines 1, 3) - You expected German, but instead you got English and French. This was easy, since the English remains the same. But more often than not this kind of "linguistic inconsistency" will require judgment calls on your part that will test your mettle as a translator.

Die Oper der Opern (line 5) - Literally translated, it would read "the opera of operas." The translator chose "The opera to end all operas," a legitimate variation. This kind of text is open to interpretation, but it should be done intelligently.

melodienselig (line 5) - Another hard-to-translate German expression.

"Musikdramas" (line 20) - Although "musical drama" is a correct general translation, "music-drama" is a coined term referring specifically to the works of Wagner.

apportieren (line 26) - Retrieved, fetched, or pulled, this is a case of a hard-to-translate word. A knowledge of the subject matter will guide you to the right synonym.

These are but a few examples of the nature of this particular text. We do hope you like opera, in which case struggling with this text may be fun.

1 Introduction

1.1 Purpose

In accordance with Item III.8 of the Administrative Regulations for the implementation of the authority extended to Deutsche Bundespost TELEKOM to exercise network monopoly of the Federal Government dated September 19, 1991 (hereinafter called "Network Monopoly Administrative Regulation") and in accordance with Item IX.8 of the Administrative Regulation for the implementation of the authority extended to Deutsche Bundespost TELEKOM to exercise the telephone service monopoly of the Federal Government dated July 13, 1992 (hereinafter called "Telephone Service Monopoly Administrative Regulation"),

"customer information which Deutsche Bundespost TELEKOM obtains from the monopoly sector may only be used for the purpose of competition to the extent that the information is available to the competitors. The corresponding regulations of the Data Protection Law remain unaffected."

1.2 Mandate

The resulting mandates for Deutsche Bundespost TELEKOM are:

• in accordance with Item IX.8 of the Telephone Service Monopoly Administrative Regulation

"Deutsche Bundespost TELEKOM is obligated to immediately present the Federal Minister for Post and Telecommunications with a concept which discloses how the TELEKOM intends to prevent the misuse of customer information obtained from the monopoly sector. If the Minister is not presented with a concept at that time or if the concept does not meet the necessary requirements, the Federal Minister for Post and Telecommunications reserves the right to demand a different concept."

• in accordance with Item III.8 of the Network Monopoly Administrative Regulation

"Deutsche Bundespost TELEKOM is obligated to present the Federal Minister for Post and Telecommunications with a concept by June 30, 1992 which discloses how TELEKOM intends to prevent the misuse of customer information obtained from the monopoly sector."

In accordance with the above Administrative Regulations, the mandates intend to create "equal opportunity" in the addressed sectors between the Deutsche Bundespost TELEKOM as a competitor and private users."

1.3 Position of TELEKOM

☐ **TELEKOM is bound by the principle of fair competition with regard to the use of monopoly services and the law of competition.**

☐ **TELEKOM is determined to guarantee a non-discriminatory use of customer information which is obtained from the monopoly sector.**

1.4 Initial Situation

In accordance with the public mandate stipulated in § 1 PostVerfG [Postal Decree Law], Deutsche Bundespost TELEKOM is required to provide infrastructure services (monopoly- and standard services) and to secure the necessary infrastructure, industrial and entrepreneurial tasks of the telecommunication services in the national and international sector.[sic] Deutsche Bundespost TELEKOM provides both monopoly and competitive services.

This makes it possible for TELEKOM to economically use facilities while taking the principles of § 37 section 4 PostVerfG (cross subsidies) into account.

1.5 Development to Date

Immediately after the Network and Telephone Service Monopoly Administrative Regulations were issued, TELEKOM initiated the necessary studies in accordance with the above described mandate. It soon became obvious that the term "customer information" was not sufficient to describe the problems which arise in this area and to fulfill TELEKOM's obligations with regard to equal opportunity. By mutual agreement with the BMPT [Federal Ministry for Post and Telecommunications], TELEKOM substituted the term "customer information" with the more suitable term "monopoly information".

1.5.1 Organizational Consequences Based on Administrative Regulations

1) A new department which, among other things, is responsible for "Competition Neutrality and Equal Opportunity in the Monopoly Sectors" was established at the corporate level of the TELEKOM. This department must directly report to the board of directors. Due to certain events, the responsibilities of this department were expanded by "Contact for questions concerning the non-discriminatory use of monopoly services by TELEKOM."

2) An independent office which is assigned to the monopoly sectors was established at the telephone exchanges. One of the most important tasks which this office must fulfill in a non-competitive manner is the "non-discriminatory supply of port and transmission path related data" as well as the corresponding maintenance of the inventory data concerning monopoly transmission paths.

Since this office is obliged to practice neutrality as far as competition is concerned, the function is directly reported to the corporate level of TELEKOM. The office directors are the immediate contact persons for competitors if they have reason to believe that TELEKOM does not adhere to the principles of equal opportunity.

3)   TELEKOM stated that, within the framework of the "TELEKOM Contact" project during the reorganization of the long-distance exchanges, the required competition neutrality would be ensured through corresponding organizational changes in the field organization.

1.5.2 Non-Discriminatory use of Monopoly Information

In this context, the above described office is responsible for the following:

Customer contacts, contacting customers in writing, neutral customer information in the monopoly sector, supply of monopoly information, non-discriminatory monopoly data transfer to the BAPT [Federal Office of Post and Telecommunications] branches, non-discriminatory measures if the regulations of the EU [European Union] are violated, if TK [TELEKOM] Facilities do not correspond to the basic requirements of the EU, competition-neutral treatment of customer orders and acceptance of orders, if competitors have a justified interest in the confidential treatment of information of their own customers as well as equal information on products of the competitive sectors due to measures in monopoly areas (e.g., when switching exchanges are used).

1.5.3 Supplying Monopoly Information to Improve Equal Opportunity Among Competitors

For this purpose it is already possible to obtain data about telephone customers ("telephone book data") and zoning data from TELEKOM. The supply of length data for monopoly transmission paths is in preparation. Activation dates of digital local switching centers can be retrieved from Vtx service.

In this context the concept of Deutsche Bundespost TELEKOM to provide open network access which would provide monopoly information to the public and would have extensive national economic importance, should be considered one of the functions of the telephone network.

The measures implemented to date are the basis for the concept, and consequently will be further developed within the concept and partially already were - partly independently of the content of the Administrative Regulations - developed together with the BMPT (Federal Ministry for Post and Telecommunications) immediately after the first post reform and were introduced to the relevant trade associations.

General comments:

a.   Subject matter

This text represents a specific area of law, namely, business or industrial law as it applies to a business agreement or contract. With this in mind, one should be sensitive to the requirements of legal translation, which means careful attention not only to the text but all the small details that go along with it, as will be explained in the examples below. Here a good German-English legal dictionary would be most useful.

b.   Format

We draw your attention to the fact that the original text is typed in a legal text format, following established form. Therefore, the English translation was formatted to look like the original, and each page of translation corresponds exactly to each page of the original. This was done for several good reasons: (a) an end-user of a translation would often need to compare the two texts, and this exact replication makes it very easy to compare, and also to make sure nothing is missing; (b) it helps the translator to check his/her own work, making sure nothing was left out; and (c) it conveys the sense of orderliness and accuracy which is critical in legal documents.

Deutsche Bundespost TELEKOM (line 7-8) - The name of the company is left in German, since it is a legal entity registered under this name. Notice also that the capitalization is preserved to match the original.

im folgenden (line 9) - "Hereinafter" is a common legal term which should be used routinely in translating legal documents.

Konkretisierung (line 10) - Translated as "implementation," it actually means more than just implementing, and perhaps "concretization" might come closer. However, the term used is more commonly used in business and legal language, and therefore was chosen over the other.

Aufträge (line 21) - This term is used here ambiguously, since the way it reads, these would be mandates issued by TELEKOM. Instead, these are orders or instructions levelled against TELEKOM. This may require a Translator's Note attached to the translation for the sake of clarity.

verpflichtet (line 25) - "Obligated" can also be used, or even "tasked."

PostVerG (page 24, line 11) - Here, as in the rest of this text, an expansion of the acronym is provided **in brackets.** Unlike parenthesis, which is part of the original text, the brackets denote extraneous material, added by the translator for the sake of elucidation.

Generaldirektion TELEKOM (line 33) - Translated as "corporate level." One could argue for a more specific translation, such as Directorate-General, although the former seems more commonly used. Also, this particular sentence is a good example of how a German sentence often requires rigorous rearranging to make it sound like English.

Additional observations:

Since legal documents such as business agreements contain a fairly standard text, you may want to get hold of one or more texts of such English-language agreements, to familiarize yourself with the style and terminology. Clearly, one does not always have the time and means to obtain this kind of information, but if this is a subject you expect to translate fairly regularly, it is worth the effort.

Also, it is important to know the purpose of a particular translation, although a translator is not always given this information by the client. If it is to be used as a legally binding agreement, it has to be accurate to the point of being accepted as a legal contract. On the other hand, if it is only for information purposes - say the end-user in this case does not read German - then you need not spend nearly as much time and effort to make sure every single word is the best possible equivalent of the original.

Introduction

The object of the Chemical Substances Act is the protection of man and environment from hazardous chemicals. When the Chemical Substances Act became effective in 1982, the tests considered essential for recognizing the toxic potential of a substance were compiled, and detailed general testing specifications were drafted, which since then have been revised with more precision or have been improved.

The experience that the Chemicals Evaluation Department was able to gain during the 12 years since the Chemical Substances Act became effective, has led to the development of suggestions for substance-specific testing strategies, resulting in a more specific toxicological evaluation, including lower expenditure of lab animals, of new base level chemicals of the Chemical Substances Act. This was published in the Activity Report of the Federal Office of Health 1991 [1]. The suggestions form one of the bases for developing new testing strategies by the working group "Further Development of Toxicological Testing Methods within the Scope of the Chemical Substances Act."

The following introduces the evaluation results of the documents on the new chemicals according to the Chemical Substances Act, related to the assessment of acute toxicity, and the specific suggestions for a procedure to determine acute dermal toxicity with low animal expenditure.

Evaluation of Reporting Documents for Chemicals with > 95% Purity

In accordance with the reporting process as stipulated by the Chemical Substances Act, in excess of 1,000 different substances have been filed EU-wide until mid-1993 in more than 2,000 reporting processes. By August 1993, a total of 1012 different chemicals had been filed:

- 532 substances can be considered pure chemicals since they contain less than 5% contaminations, and these contaminations are not relevant for the toxic properties considered here.
- 480 substances are mixtures of different chemical substances.

Since the Chemical Substances Act prescribes detailed physico-chemical and toxicological testing documents for assessing physico-chemical substance properties and toxic substance effects for new chemicals using standardized testing methods, the Chemical Evaluation Department thus possesses substance data preparations that are complete and have been tested by the authorities during the filing process for all new substances filed EU-wide; these data sets can be directly compared with each other.

To find the connections between the physico-chemical substance properties, on the one hand, and the acutely toxic, locally irritating and skin-sensitizing substance effects, on the other hand, the testing documents of 345 pure chemicals were evaluated with the help of individual examples.

The objective is the development of computerized structure-effect models (SAR-models) to predict acutely toxic, locally irritating and skin-sensitizing substance effects [2].

Of 345 studied chemicals, a total of 163 (47.2%) are categorized as acutely toxic, locally irritating, or skin-sensitizing and were marked with the appropriate hazard identifications (R-Notes):

- 80 substances (23.2%) as locally irritating or corrosive to the eye,
- 74 substances (21.5%) as skin-sensitizing,
- 65 substances (18.8%) as orally less toxic or toxic,
- 55 substances (15.9%) as locally irritating or corrosive to skin,
- 8 substances (2.3%) as dermally less toxic or toxic.

A more detailed analysis of the acutely toxic and locally irritating effects of the studied substances that were subject to identification showed the following results [3]:

- Oral administration of corrosive substances very frequently, but in no case always, results in the death of the test animals; Of the 20 corrosive substances found, five have an oral LD50 >2,000 mg/kg.
- Dermal application only very rarely has an acutely toxic effect.
- The dermally acutely toxic substances investigated must in no case be marked exclusively because of this single toxic effect; but all 8 dermally acutely toxic substances also have an orally acutely toxic effect and additionally exhibit local corrosive effects with distinct clinical toxicity symptoms (Table 1, substances 1-8).   However, of those substances that were evaluated as neither orally toxic nor locally irritating, no substance exhibited any kind of classification-relevant acute dermal toxicity.
- By far not all substances classified as strong skin irritants also have a strong irritating effect on the eyes.
- Although many substances produce serious eye injuries, they do not or only insignificantly irritate the skin.

Predictability of Acute Dermal Toxicity

The previous evaluation of testing documents according to the Chemical Substances Act has shown that it should be possible to predict whether the application of a chemical substance to the skin of test animals could lead to the death of said animals within 14 days. The overview of certain physico-chemical substance data [4-8] and observations during the test regarding acute oral toxicity and local irritations to skin and eyes should be able to indicate whether a substance is able to penetrate the skin in such a relevant amount that acute distinct clinical symptoms or a classification-relevant LD50 would have to be expected. Animal experiments to determine the acute dermal LD50 would then be required only for those very few chemicals whose acute dermal toxicity could not be predicted theoretically with the required certainty.

Table 1 (substances 1-8) shows that all dermally acutely toxic substances that were found not only have a dermal but also an additional oral acutely toxic effect. Furthermore, they all cause skin and/or eye burns, and, in addition to the burn effects, also cause distinct toxicity symptoms (corresponding systemic effects were observed in Draize tests).

It can also be seen that these chemicals have a relatively good solubility in water, since the evaluations show that for acutely toxic substance effects only a solubility of <1.0 g/l should be considered as "poorly water-soluble." Seven of the eight substances also are relatively readily soluble in fat ("poor solubility in fat" for acutely toxic effects are solubilities of <0.1 g/kg).

Substance No.4 is remarkable in many respects: It exhibits poor solubility in fat and thus does not irritate skin [3] ; it has an unusually low oral LD50 of 150 mg/kg and thus must be labelled "orally toxic"; and it causes more than eye burns -- during the eye irritation test, two of the three test animals died within 48 hours.

General comments:

This is a scientific chemical paper which requires not only direct translation into English, but also a careful revision of one's translation to achieve good English readability, in view of the length and complexity of many of the sentences. The following examples show some of the pitfalls of the material, and you may want to check and see how they match your own "rough spots" in doing this particular assignment. A good German-English chemical dictionary would certainly be very helpful, but one also needs a general understanding of the subject-matter and be familiar with this kind of writing.

Die Erfahrungen...sind [1] (lines 11-15) - This is one long complex sentence that is hard to render into clear and simple English. One cannot replicate the original word for word and come up with a satisfactory translation. Rather, it is necessary to edit the text, which includes breaking this long sentence into two or more sentences so as to achieve a smoothly flowing, intelligible English translation.

Reinheit >95% (line 25) - One may be tempted to translate this term as Purity >95%, when the correct form is either ">95% Purity" or "Purity of >95%."

gekennzeichnet (page 27, line 9) - One may choose to translate "identified," when the correct translation is "marked."

oral mindegiftig (line 13) - What seems like "oral minor toxicity," translates correctly into English as "orally less toxic."

"schlecht wasserlöslich" (page 28, line 9) - "Poorly soluble" won't do; one needs to specify "water-soluble."

Sieben der acht (line 9) - At the beginning of the sentence, Arabic numerals are spelled out.

A successful first step in Guatemala

In January 1992, Empresa Eléctrica de Guatemala S.A. (EEGSA) - the major power distributor in Guatemala - signed a fifteen-year power purchase agreement with a local power-generating company. Almost immediately the company sold its interest in the project to Enron Power Development Corporation, a subsidiary of a large U.S. natural gas company with interests in several independent power projects. The project consists of twenty 5.5-megawatt generators mounted on a barge at Puerto Quetzal, which operate as a base-load plant. The project increases Guatemala's generating capacity by 12 percent and its effective capacity by about 15 percent.

The prices in the power purchase agreement are denominated in U.S. dollars. The agreement requires EEGSA to provide the project company, Puerto Quetzal Power Corporation (PQP), with weekly fixed capacity payments, provided that PQP meets minimum availability standards; weekly energy payments, with a minimum guaranteed purchase of 50 percent of output; and additional collateral and documentary support to secure EEGSA's obligations to PQP. EEGSA has the option to pay PQP in U.S. dollars or quetzales at the prevailing market rate. When power availability falls below 50 percent, PQP will pay EEGSA penalties. The agreement requires the project to provide power at a competitive price. Under current assumptions of capacity utilization, which allow for deterioration of performance over time, EEGSA will pay an average of $0.07 per kilowatt-hour over the life of the project-which is about the long-run marginal cost of bulk power in Guatemala.

PQP has cut some of its risks by entering into contracts for turnkey installation, operations and maintenance, and fuel supply. The plant started operating in late February 1993, on schedule and within budget. A review of early operations indicates that PQP has achieved high levels of available capacity, that revenues and net income agree with forecasts, and that converting quetzales into U.S. dollars has not been a problem. After watching EEGSA's experience with PQP, the Instituto Nacional de Electrificación - a government-owned enterprise responsible for power generation, transmission, and retail distribution outside Guatemala City - has begun negotiating other power purchase agreements with independent producers.

Mexico's toll roads: a big push that faltered

Infrastructure projects are often associated with large construction outlays that result in limited productive use. This can occur as much under private as under public enterprise if the right incentives are not in place.

In preparation for an ambitious 6,000-kilometer road program, a Mexican government agency did hasty traffic and cost projections and prepared the road designs. The quality of these estimates and designs fell far short of requirements for such an undertaking. At the same time, state-owned banks lending to toll-road projects did not perform the normal project screening and appraisals.

Although the concessions for road construction and operation were awarded based on several criteria, investors who promised to transfer the roads back to the government in the shortest time were especially favored. Short concessions were partly motivated by a concern that only short-term financing would be available. The attempt to achieve success within a new administration's term also created a sense of urgency. In turn, investors negotiated toll rates that would earn a return within the concession period. Tolls typically were therefore five to ten times higher than those in the United States for comparable distances.

With tolls that high, traffic failed to materialize-the old, free roads were preferred even when travel time was typically twice as long. Moreover, cost overruns averaged more than 50 percent of projected costs. (The Highway of the Sun, from Cuernavaca to Acapulco, for example, cost $2.1 billion, more than twice the original estimate.)

To remedy the situation, the Mexican government has taken several steps. In many cases, concession periods have been extended from ten or fifteen years to thirty years. Where joint ventures offer greater prospects of financial viability, stretches of toll road are being combined under single management. Heavier vehicles may be banned from the old road network as weight limits are imposed and enforced.

There are signs that the most difficult period is past. In the long run, consolidations of toll roads, longer concession periods, and more realistic traffic and cost projections, along with economic growth and greater financial responsibility on the part of the project's private sponsor, should bring significant returns on this infrastructure investment.

Leveraging through guarantees in Thailand

To encourage private lending, the Thai government is developing the Thai Guaranty Facility to guarantee loans made by private financial institutions to municipalities and private operators of urban environmental infrastructure. The facility is planned as a public-private corporation with private sector management. The target date for initial operation of the facility is June 1994.

Because of limited experience in lending to municipalities, financial institutions consider them risky borrowers. Perceiving high project risks, lenders are reluctant to make loans for periods of longer than eight years-too short to recoup investment from environmental infrastructure.

By providing guarantees to private operators and municipalities that help them to secure loans from commercial lenders, the government's guaranty facility will create longer-term financing. With increased lending to local government, it will soon be possible to establish credit ratings for cities and to allow them to issue bonds. Ten provincial cities, the five cities of the Bangkok Metropolitan Region, and Bangkok itself are expected to be the primary beneficiaries of loan guarantees for investments in wastewater treatment, solid waste collection and disposal, and potable water supply.

During its first two years of operation, the guaranty facility is expected to receive $75 million. Lending will be five to eight times the level of these guaranty funds. Over a five-year period, it is projected that the facility will be funded at a level of $150 million and will leverage up to $1.2 billion in loans for urban environmental infrastructure projects. It will obtain resources principally from the Thai government, from money borrowed in part from the USAID Housing Guaranty Program and in part from Thai financial institutions.

A set of policy initiatives is also being established to ensure the effectiveness of this facility, including a move toward the "polluter-pays" principle, changes in administrative procedures, and greater decentralization of decisionmaking.

General comments:

a. Financial Translation

In translation, there is a basic difference between translating financial subjects and other technical subjects, such as legal or medical. While it is relatively easy to master the methodology of working with most technical vocabularies, even if one does not have the technical or professional background of the particular field in which one translates, in financial subjects it is necessary to have at least a general knowledge of the subject. This may be due to the fact that financial terminology and concepts are not always as readily translatable as other technical subjects. The upshot of all this is that one should not be hasty to accept a financial translation assignment if one does not work in this field on a regular basis.

b. Subject matter

This particular assignment consists of three texts derived from a publication of an international financial organization. As with most major organizations and corporations, this organization has its own so-called "corporate style," which affects the way this material is translated. Normally, an organization of this magnitude employs its own translators, or uses outside translators on a regular basis, to acquaint them with its style. If called upon to translate this kind of text, be sure to familiarize yourself with the organization's style.

Empresa Eléctrica de Guatemala S.A. (line 6) - The name of the Guatemalan national electric company remains untranslated, because it is a legal entity registered under this name. In a newspaper article, for instance, the name would most likely be translated into English, but in a document related to an international financial institution it has to remain untranslated.

wichtigste (line 6) - Translated as "the major," one could argue for "most important" as being more accurate, but "the major" sounds better.

Kraftwerksgesellschaft (line 8) - One could argue for "power plant company," but "power-generating company" does not change the meaning.

5,5-Megawatt (line 11) - The comma in German decimals changes into period in English.

fünfzehn Jahren (page 30, line 36) - Here numbers are spelled out, rather than rendered by Arabic numerals. Be sure in doing technical - particularly financial - translations that you have an understanding with your client as to what numbering system they prefer, since conventions vary with each client and institution.

Entscheidungsprozeß (page 31, line 38) - Here we have "decisionmaking" as one word, not a common usage in English, yet obviously favored by a major international financial institution.

This is an example of "corporate language," or "corporate-speak," which is very wide-spread in American business and other areas of American activities.

Part Two

Translation : English into German

Origin and Structure

5   The Smithsonian owes its origin to James Smithson, an English scientist who never visited the United States but who nevertheless willed his entire fortune to this country "to found at Washington, under the name of the Smithsonian Institution, an Establishment for the increase and diffusion of knowledge among men."

10   Smithson died in Italy in 1829, and his bequest of more than half a million dollars - a great fortune in that day - was received with mixed feelings in Washington in 1838, stirring up a lengthy debate in Congress as to whether the nation should, or indeed could, legally accept the funds and accompanying trust. After studying the matter for eight years, Congress decided to accept the bequest, but also determined that the federal government lacked the authority to

15   administer such a trust directly. As a result, it created a corporate entity, "The Establishment," to take charge of the Smithson will. This body, in effect constituting the Smithsonian Institution, consisted of the President of the United States, the Vice President, the Chief Justice, and the heads of the executive departments. To actually govern the Institution, a board of regents was created, along with the position of Secretary of the Smithsonian.

20

The Smithsonian bequest was deposited in the United States Treasury and the government agreed to pay 6 percent interest on it to the Smithsonian in perpetuity. In the formal creation of the Smithsonian, provision was made for work in areas that have continued to be of concern - science, art, history, research, museum and library operation, and the dissemination of

25   information.

In taking action on Smithson's bequest, Congress said that its purpose was to provide for "the faithful execution of said trust agreeable to the will of the liberal and enlightened donor." In this way, the United States Government solemnly bound itself to the administration of a trust, and the

30   relation of the government to the Smithsonian became as a guardian to a ward.

Thus the Smithsonian today is a national institution that receives substantial support from the federal government as well as essential funding from private sources, including the Smithson endowment. Control rests in the Board of Regents, which is composed of the Chief Justice of the

35   United States, the Vice President, three members each from the Senate and the House of Representatives, and nine private citizens. The board elects the Secretary of the Smithsonian, who is the administrative head of the Institution. Included under the aegis of the Smithsonian, but separately administered by their own boards of trustees are the **National Gallery of Art** (see page 19), the **Woodrow Wilson International Center for Scholars**, and the **John F. Kennedy**

40   **Center for the Performing Arts**. The Wilson Center, located in the Smithsonian Building, was

established by Congress in 1968 as a living memorial to President Woodrow Wilson and serves as an international institute for advanced study. The Kennedy Center, on Rock Creek Parkway at New Hampshire Avenue and F Street NW, was created by Congress in 1958 as the National Cultural Center, and was designated in 1964 as a memorial to the late President Kennedy.

The Castle

The red sandstone Smithsonian Institution Building, with its eight crenelated towers, symbolizes the entire Institution to many visitors. Popularly known as the Castle, it was designed in Norman style by James Renwick, Jr., architect of Grace Church and Saint Patrick's Cathedral in New York and the Renwick Gallery in Washington (see page 137).

In the beginning, the Castle housed all the Smithsonian's operations, including a science museum, lecture hall, art gallery, research laboratories and administrative offices, and living quarters for the Secretary and his family. Today, the Castle is largely used for the Institution's administrative offices, including the Secretary's. It is also the home of the Woodrow Wilson International Center for Scholars.

Western Civilization: Origins and Traditions

This exhibit traces the increasing complexity of Western civilization from the end of the Ice Age, about 10,000 years ago, to about A.D. 500. Ice Age flint tools, such as knives and projectile points, and a reconstructed cave featuring paintings of animals illustrate man's early dependence on hunting.

It was after the Ice Age that people in southwestern Asia began the shift to farming as a way of life. A scene from one of the earliest farming villages - Ali Kosh - is re-created in a diorama. Technological advances accompanied the spread of agriculture. Egyptian pottery from 4000 B.C. is shown, along with increasingly sophisticated stone and bone tools from Europe. Another diorama re-creates a scene from the Mesopotamian city of Larsa in 1801 B.C.

The growing complexity of urban life fostered a new form of political and social organization called the "state," which eventually led to the formation of empires.

The growth of empires is illustrated with an outstanding collection of artifacts, including pottery and stone tools from Troy, Luristan bronzes, Egyptian mummies and mummy cases, a Cycladic figurine, Etruscan bronzes, Greek pottery, Roman glass, a Roman mosaic, and Roman money.

By about A.D. 500, the basic patterns of Western civilization were set, and many of them persist today. The last part of the hall focuses on this persistence, with a reconstructed modern bazaar scene, a comparison of a Roman cookbook with a modern one, and a fascinating film on the town of Winchester, England, from its Celtic origins through Roman occupation to the present.

word count: 882

5   The foregoing provisions and the other provisions of this Agreement relating to the maintenance of Capital Accounts are intended to comply with Regulations Section 1.704-1(b), and shall be interpreted and applied in a manner consistent with such Regulations. In the event the General Partner shall determine that it is prudent to modify the manner in which the Capital Accounts, or any debits or credits thereto, are computed in order to comply with such Regulations, the General

10 Partner may make such modification, provided that it is not likely to have a material effect on the amounts distributable to any Partner or Holder of Units pursuant to Section 8 hereof upon the dissolution of the Partnership.

15 1.10.   "**Capital Contribution**" in respect of any General Partner or Holder of Units, including any Limited Partner, means the amount of all cash contributed (whether by original contributions, or otherwise) by such Holder of Units and any predecessor in interest of such Holder of Units to the capital of the Partnership. Also included is the initial Gross Asset Value contributed to the Partnership by a Partner.

20 1.11.   "**Capital Transaction**" means an Interim Capital Transaction and/or a Terminating Capital Transaction.

1.12.   "**Cash Flow**" means cash funds from all sources (not including Capital Contributions, loan proceeds, Interim and Terminating Capital Transactions), without deduction for depreciation

25 or amortization, but after deducting cash funds used to pay all other expenses, debt payments, capital improvements and replacements and to create or restore reserves.

1.13.   "**Code**" means the Internal Revenue code of 1986, as amended (or any corresponding provisions of succeeding law).

30

1.14.   "**Commission**" means the Securities and Exchange Commission.

1.15.   "**Depreciation**" means, for each fiscal year or other period, an amount equal to the depreciation, amortization, or other cost recovery deduction allowable with respect to an asset for

35 such year or other period, except that if the Gross Asset Value of an asset differs from its adjusted basis for federal income tax purposes at the beginning of such year or other period, Depreciation shall be an amount which bears the same ratio to such beginning Gross Asset Value as the federal income tax depreciation, amortization, or other cost recovery deduction for such year or other period bears to such beginning adjusted tax basis: provided however that if the

40 federal income tax depreciation, amortization, or other cost recovery deduction for such year is zero, depreciation shall be determined with reference to such beginning Gross Asset Value using any reasonable method selected by the General Partner.

1.16.   "**General Partner**" means the person(s) designated as "General Partner" in the signature block at the end of this Agreement or a corporation or business entity made up of the same individuals as any substitutes as provided by this Agreement.   The named General Partner(s) may at their sole discretion and without the approval of the Limited partners, add more, or delete some persons as General Partners (but this shall not change the General Partners' interest, duties, or responsibilities).

1.17.   "**Gross Asset Value**" means, with respect to any asset, as determined by the contributing Partner and the Partnership;

1.17.1 The initial Gross Asset Value of ant asset contributed by a Partner to the Partnership shall be the gross fair market value of such asset, as determined by the contributing Partner and the Partnership;

1.17.2 The Gross Asset Values of all Partnership assets shall be adjusted to equal their respective gross fair market values, as determined by the General Partner, as of the following times: (a) the acquisition of an additional interest in the Partnership by any new or existing Partner in exchange for more than a *de minimis* Capital Contribution; (b) the distribution by the Partnership to a Partner or a Holder of Units of more than a *de minimis* amount of Partnership Property as consideration for an interest in the Partnership; and (c) the liquidation of the Partnership within the meaning of Regulations Section 1.704-1(b)(2)(ii)(g); provided, however, that the adjustments pursuant to clauses (a) and (b) above shall be made only if the General Partner reasonably determines that such adjustments are necessary or appropriate to reflect the relative economic interests of the Partners and Holders of Units in the Partnership;

1.17.3 The Gross Asset Value of any Partnership asset distributed to any Partner or Holder of Units shall be the gross fair market value of such asset on the date of distribution; and

1.17.4 The Gross Asset Values of Partnership assets shall be increased (or decreased) to reflect any adjustments to the adjusted basis of such assets pursuant Code Section 734(b) or Code Section 743(b), but only to the extent that such adjustments are taken into account in determining Capital Accounts pursuant to Regulations Section 1.704-1(b)(2)(iv)(m).

If the Gross Asset Value of an asset has been determined or adjusted pursuant to this Section, such Gross Asset Value shall thereafter be adjusted by the Depreciation taken into account with respect to such asset for purposes of computing Profits and Losses.

1.18.   "**Holder of Units**" means those persons or entities which from time to time are shown the books and records of the Partnership as being owners of Units, whether or not such persons or entities have been admitted to the Partnership as Limited Partners.

1.19.   "**Interim Capital Transaction**" means any of the following events: (i) the sale of part of the Property; (ii) the recovery of insurance proceeds or other damage recoveries by the Partnership in respect of a casualty loss exceeding the cost of restoration; (iii) the

5 receipt of proceeds from condemnation of part of the Property; and (iv) the refinancing of loans to the Partnership or the original acquisition of debt financing, to the extent that the proceeds are not applied to expenses incurred in the repair or restoration of the Property, or set aside for or applied to the payment of liabilities relating to the acquisition, improvement or operation of the Property.

10 1.20. "**Land**" means any real property owned by the Partnership at any time.

word count: 981

5   **Discussion**

The goal of our survey was, on the one hand, to record the scope of different bone grafts, especially allogeneic grafts, in the Federal Republic of Germany and, on the other, to indicate the differences in the bone bank logistics. The selection criteria of the clinics surveyed were
10   determined by the size and the functions of the clinics. Since bone banking requires significant technology, extensive funding and extra personnel, hospitals with fewer than 60 surgical beds, or clinics which do not have a trauma center (according to "Deutsche Chirurgie '88" [13]) were not included in the survey.

15   The high return rate of 46.4% of the questionnaires leads to the conclusion that the questions in the questionnaire were considered to be significant. It was possible to survey surgical clinics with a total of approximately 39,000 beds.

Table 2. Examinations of the bone donor before allogeneic grafting at 209 clinics

	Yes		No	
	n	%	n	%
Hepatitis B	184	88	21	10
HIV	174	83	31	15
Lues	162	78	43	21
Bacteriology qual.	155	74	50	24
Rhesus factor	61	29	134	64
Histology	48	23	157	75
Blood types	45	22	152	73
Bacteriology quant.	45	22	160	77
Bacteriology as intermediate analysis	26	12	179	86
Cytomegalic disease	12	6	193	92
Malaria	1	0.5	204	98

20
The ratio of the clinics which do not conduct any bone grafts to those which conduct only autogenous or both autogenous and allogeneic bone grafts is in itself interesting. Only 5% of the clinics conducted no bone grafts, 39% used only autogenous, and 45% used allogenic bone grafts

as well. This means that in the survey year 1987, allogeneic bone was transplanted 6,000 times in 209 clinics.

5 Taking into account that about 50% of the clinics did not respond, and that orthopedic clinics were not included (21,500 beds according to the Statistisches Bundesamt [Federal Statistical Office] in Wiesbaden in 1987), it seems reasonable to estimate that approximately 15,000 allogeneic bone grafts are conducted annually in the Federal Republic of Germany. Despite the high number of grafts conducted, no coherent concept for bone bank techniques can be deduced from the answers provided in the questionnaires. For this reason we would like to comment only 10 on the few items in the survey where the variance of the results speaks for itself.

What was striking with regard to donor examinations was that no serological tests on transmittable viral diseases and no bacterial examinations were conducted in approximately 25% of the clinics. In light of the proof that allogeneic bone preserved by refrigeration can transmit 15 bacterial as well as viral diseases (especially HIV, [6, 10]), it is unacceptable - from a medical as well as a legal point of view - that these tests are not conducted.

Blood types were not a factor in 73% and Rh factors in 64% of the cases. This is very critical since there are causal connections for the formation of antibodies - at least as regards Rh factors 20 - in young women [9, 10, 12] after Rh-incompatible bone grafts. Studies we conducted also prove that even in ABO-systems, recipients can form antibodies after incompatible bone grafts. In pregnant women this can result in the formation of a morbid hemolytic disease of the newborn [11]. At the present time, the guidelines of the scientific advisory board of the Bundesärztekammer [Federal Medical Association] do not stipulate mandatory consideration of 25 Rh systems or of ABO-blood types [17].

Considerable differences can also be found in the treatment, packaging and storage of grafts. The packaging must ensure that there is no secondary contamination. Single packaging in plastic bags, which can easily be damaged, does not provide this protection. 30

Evidently, there are considerable differences regarding the indications for adding local antibiotics or disinfecting agents to the allogeneic graft. While 72 clinics conduct a local adjuvant antibiotics therapy, the majority of the clinics have no such regimen.

35 The storage temperature and the storage period, as well as the type of packaging, are indications as to the extent to which allogeneic bone is classified in accordance with the requirements of a biological transplant. Single packaging at a storage temperature of -18°C does not meet the requirements of a biological transplant [3, 15]. Maximum storage of up to five years seems to be questionable as regards the biological quality of the graft in addition to the possibility of 40 bacterial contamination [3].

Some clinics discontinued allogeneic grafts due to AIDS. On the other hand, other clinics did not even introduce HIV serology because of AIDS, even with the donor's written consent - which is mandatory. Also, the second HIV test was conducted in only a few cases. There is evidence 45 that hepatitis and bacterial diseases - even more so than HIV infections - are transmitted through allogeneic grafts. This is why it is equally worrisome that these more common diseases are not screened in 10 - 24 % of the donations and thus can be transmitted to the recipients.

The possibility that tumorous diseases can also be transmitted does not seem to affect the bone bank techniques of many clinics, since 75 % of them do not conduct any histological tests on the grafts.

5

The results of the survey confirm that despite numerous publications on allogeneic grafts or bone bank systems in the Federal Republic of Germany, there is a wide range of different bone bank systems some of which can no longer be reconciled with new findings and recommendations. There is no standardization. Allogeneic grafts must be treated the same way as organ transplants and must be carried out under the same strict criteria with regard to donor and recipient selection as well as transplant storage. Based on medical and legal considerations, uniform management of bone bank techniques is imperative.

10

We would like to express our gratitude to all clinics which actively participated in our survey.

15

word count: 889

ASSIGNMENT 4: FINANCE

5   THE NEED FOR NEW APPROACHES. In the coming decade, demand for infrastructure investments will simultaneously increase in two different sets of countries: those that have undertaken macroeconomic adjustment with consequent low investment levels and, at the other extreme, those whose rapid growth is now placing a heavy burden on infrastructure. Infrastructure investments in developing countries represent, on average, 4 percent of GDP, but

10   they often need to be substantially higher. Where telecommunications or power-supply networks are expanding rapidly, annual investments in either sector can be as high as 2 percent of GDP. A special factor increasing investment demand in many countries is the rapid pace of urbanization, requiring investments in water supply as well as waste treatment and disposal.

15   In Asia, the share of infrastructure investment in GDP is expected to rise from 4 percent today to more than 7 percent by the turn of the century, with transport and energy likely to demand the most resources, followed by telecommunications and environmental infrastructure. Some of the planned investments are without precedent. China, for example, has set a target of installing at least 5 million telephone lines annually up to 1995 and at least 8 million lines per year thereafter,

20   to more than triple its 1992 base of 18 million lines by the year 2000.

Private entrepreneurship: trends and opportunities

Current efforts to secure increased private sponsorship and risktaking in infrastructure projects

25   reflect these various challenges. After decades of severe regulatory restriction, private entrepreneurship in infrastructure bounced back in two ways during the late 1980s: through the privatization of state-owned utilities and through policy reform that made possible the construction of new facilities in competition with, or as a complement to, existing enterprises.

30   The principal new infrastructure entrepreneurs are international firms seeking business in developing countries and operating often in association with local companies. These firms bring to bear not only their management expertise and technical skills, but also their credit standing and ability to finance investments in developing countries. Major electric, telecommunications, and water utilities in industrial countries face slowly growing demand and increased competition

35   (following deregulation) in their home markets. As a result, they are vigorously seeking high-yielding investments in developing countries. Construction conglomerates are active in toll-road construction and in power projects, where they sometimes take an equity interest. Some companies or groups of companies also specialize in stand-alone infrastructure projects, putting together financing packages and overseeing project development and operation.

40

Most indicators of infrastructure investment under private sponsorship reveal rapid growth. Privatized telecommunications and electricity utilities in Latin America and Asia are undertaking large and growing new investments. The number of these so-called greenfield projects -- especially in the road and electric power sectors -- has grown rapidly (as discussed below). Infrastructure investments by the International Finance Corporation (IFC), a World Bank affiliate that invests only in private entities, have experienced a surge, from modest amounts in the late 1980s to $330 million in fiscal 1993. The amount invested by the IFC was leveraged more than ten times, so that, in 1993, IFC participated in private investments of $3.5 billion.

The most important development during the past four years has been the explosion in international flows of long-term private capital to developing countries, especially in the form of foreign direct investment and portfolio flows. Aggregate flows stood at more than $80 billion in 1992 and were projected to reach $112 billion in 1993 (Table 5.1). Infrastructure has been a significant beneficiary of such flows (Box 5.2).

Aggregate private investment in infrastructure in developing countries is currently about $15 billion a year, or roughly 7 percent of the $200 billion being spent annually on infrastructure in these countries. Although small, the fraction of private investment in infrastructure investment is much larger than it was some years ago, and there is a strong likelihood that private investment will continue to grow, possibly doubling its share of the total by the year 2000. One indication is the IFC's current infrastructure pipeline, which is almost as large as all the projects financed to date.

The small overall share of private finance in infrastructure obscures large regional and sectoral disparities. Private finance is proportionately greater in Latin America than in other regions, and larger in telecommunications and electric power generation than in other sectors. The diffusion of current experience across regions and sectors will raise the global share of private sponsorship and finance. For example, telecommunications privatization and independent power generation are under discussion in all regions, including Sub-Saharan Africa. And continuing technological and financial innovations will undoubtedly make private financing more attractive. As an example, electronic methods of identifying vehicles and charging tolls could make roads more like a public utility service, and boost the share of private finance in the highway sector.

Even with the rising share of privately financed infrastructure, governments will continue to be an important source of financing. Often, they will need to be partners with private entrepreneurs. Public-private partnerships in some ways represent a return to the nineteenth century, when infrastructure projects were privately financed in much of the world while government support acted as a stimulant. But the nineteenth century experience also offers important warning signs (Box 5.3)

Table 5.1 Portfolio and foreign direct investment in developing countries, 1990–93
(net inflows in billions of dollars)

Type	1990	1991	1992	1993[a]
Foreign equity securities	3.78	7.55	13.07	13.1
Closed-end funds[b]	2.78	1.20	1.34	2.7
ADRs and GDRs[c]	0.14	4.90	5.93	7.2
Direct equity	0.77	1.45	5.80	3.2
Debt instruments	5.56	12.72	23.73	42.6
Bonds	4.68	10.19	21.24	39.1
Commercial paper	0.23	1.38	0.85	1.6
Certificates of deposit	0.65	1.15	1.64	1.8
Total portfolio[d]	9.34	20.27	36.80	55.7
Foreign direct investment	26.30	36.90	47.30	56.3
Total	35.64	57.17	84.10	112.0

Note: This table records all portfolio and direct investment flows. Separate figures for infrastructure are not available.
a. 1993 figures are estimated or projected.
b. A closed-end fund has a predetermined amount of funding and sometimes a fixed life.
c. ADR = American depositary receipts; GDR = global depositary receipts. An ADR is an instrument used by an offshore company to raise equity in the United States without formal listing on a U.S. stock exchange. GDRs are similar instruments used in Europe and elsewhere.
d. Portfolio investment is the sum of equity and debt.
Source: World Bank 1993i, pp. 10, 21.

word count: 925

Ursprung und Struktur

Die Smithsonian verdankt ihre Entstehung James Smithson, einem englischen Wissenschaftler, der Amerika nie besucht hatte, ihm aber trotzdem sein gesamtes Erbe hinterließ, "um in Washington eine Einrichtung unter dem Namen Smithsonian Institution zur Erweiterung und Verbreitung von Kenntnissen unter den Menschen zu gründen".

Smithson starb 1829 in Italien, und seine Hinterlassenschaft von mehr als einer halben Million Dollar - ein großes Vermögen zu jener Zeit - wurde mit gemischten Gefühlen 1838 in Washington in Empfang genommen; es kam zu einer anhaltenden Debatte im Congress, ob die Nation die Erbschaft und die damit verbundene Treuhandschaft rechtlich akzeptieren sollte oder überhaupt könnte. Nachdem die Angelegenheit über acht Jahre lang eingehend studiert worden war, entschied der Congress, die Nachlassenschaft zu akzeptieren, bestimmte jedoch gleichzeitig, daß die Bundesregierung nicht die Befugnis habe, eine solche Stiftung selbst zu verwalten. Infolgedessen wurde eine Körperschaft gegründet, "The Establishment", die die Nachlassenschaft von Smithson übernahm. Diese Körperschaft, die in der Tat die Smithsonian Stiftung bildet, bestand aus dem Präsidenten der Vereinigten Staaten, dem Vizepräsidenten, dem vorsitzenden Richter des Obersten Bundesgerichts, den Leitern der Exekutivstellen. Für die eigentliche Verwaltung wurde ein Rat von Verwesern und das Amt des Sekretärs gegründet.

Smithsons Nachlassenschaft wurde im Schatzamt der Vereinigten Staaten deponiert und die Regierung gab ihr Einverständnis, auf ewig sechs Prozent Zinsen an die Smithsonian zu zahlen. Bei der formellen Gründung der Smithsonian wurde Vorsorge für die Arbeiten auf den Gebieten getroffen, die heute noch zu ihren Hauptaufgaben gehören: Wissenschaft, Kunst, Geschichte, Forschung, Museen, Bibliotheken und die Informationsverbreitung.

In seiner Entscheidung in bezug auf Smithsons Nachlassenschaft äußerte sich der Congress dahingehend, daß der Zweck "die gewissenhafte Vollstreckung des Testaments im Sinne des liberalen und aufgeklärten Wohltäters" sein sollte. Auf diese Weise verpflichtete sich die Regierung der Vereinigten Staaten feierlich zur Verwaltung einer Stiftung, und das Verhältnis der Regierung Smithsonian wurde das eines Vormunds zu seinem Mündel.

Somit ist die Smithsonian heute eine nationale Stiftung, die eine erhebliche Unterstützung von der Bundesregierung sowie beträchtliche Summen aus privaten Quellen einschließlich der Smithsonian Stiftung erhält. Die Kontrolle liegt beim Rat der Verweser, der aus dem vorsitzenden Richter des Obersten Bundesgerichts der Vereinigten Staaten, dem Vizepräsidenten, jeweils drei Mitgliedern des Senats und des Repräsentantenhauses der Vereinigten Staaten und neun Privatbürgern besteht. Der Rat wählt den Sekretär, der Verwaltungsleiter der Stiftung ist. Innerhalb der Smithsonian bestehen drei Körperschaften, die von ihrem eigenen Rat von Treuhändern getrennt verwaltet werden: **die Nationale Kunstgalerie** (siehe Seite 19), **das**

Internationale Woodrow Wilson Zentrum für Gelehrte und das **John F. Kennedy Zentrum für die ausübenden Künste.** Das Wilson Zentrum, das sich im ursprünglichen Gebäude der Smithsonian befindet, wurde 1968 zum Gedächtnis an Präsident Woodrow Wilson vom Congress gegründet und dient als ein internationales Institut für fortgeschrittene Studien. Das Kennedy Zentrum, am Rock Creek Parkway, der New Hampshire Avenue und F Straße NW gelegen, wurde 1958 vom Congress als Nationales Kulturzentrum geschaffen und 1964 dem Gedenken Präsident Kennedys geweiht.

Das "Schloß"

Das rote Sandsteingebäude mit seinen acht zinnenförmigen Türmen versinnbildlicht die gesamte Stiftung für viele Besucher. Allgemein als "das Schloß" bekannt, wurde es in normannischen Stil von James Renwick, Jr., dem Architekten der Grace-Kirche und der Kathedrale St. Patrick in New York und der Renwick Galerie in Washington, entworfen. (Siehe Seite 137)

Am Anfang war die ganze Smithsonian Stiftung im "Schloß" untergebracht. Sie enthielt damals ein Museum der Wissenschaften, einen Vortragssaal, eine Kunstgalerie, Forschungslaboratorien, Verwaltungsbüros und die Wohnung des Sekretärs und seiner Familie. Heute wird das "Schloß" in erster Linie für Verwaltungsbüros, einschließlich dem des Sekretärs, verwendet. Das Internationale Woodrow Wilson Zentrum für Gelehrte findet ebenfalls dort Unterkunft.

Westliche Zivilisation: Ursprung und Traditionen

Diese Ausstellung verfolgt die zunehmende Komplexität der westlichen Zivilisation vom Ende der Eiszeit vor etwa 10.000 Jahren bis etwa 500 A.D. Feuersteinwerkzeuge wie Messer und Wurfwaffenspitzen und eine nachgebildete Höhle mit Tierzeichnungen zeugen von der frühen Abhängigkeit des Menschen von der Jagd.

Nach der Eiszeit begannen die Menschen im südwestlichen Asien sich der Landwirtschaft als Lebensweise zuzuwenden. Eine Szene in einem der frühesten landwirtschaftlichen Dörfer - Ali Kosh - ist in einem Diorama nachgebildet. Zur Verbreitung der Landwirtschaft gesellte sich der Fortschritt der Technik. Neben ägyptischen Töpferwaren, die aus der Zeit von 4000 Jahren vor der Geburt Christi stammen, werden immer besser entwickelte Stein- und Knochenwerkzeuge aus Europa gezeigt. Ein anderes Diorama illustriert eine Szene aus der mesopotamischen Stadt Larsa im Jahre 1801 vor der Geburt Christi.

Die zunehmende Komplexität städtischen Lebens förderte eine neue Form der politischen und gesellschaftlichen Organisation, die "Staat" genannt wurde und schließlich zur Bildung von Kaiserreichen führte.

Diese Entwicklung wird durch eine außergewöhnliche Sammlung von Kunstwerken illustriert: Töpferwaren und Steinwerkzeuge aus Troja, luristanische Bronzen, ägyptische Mumien und ihre Särge, eine Statue von den Kykladen, etruskische Bronzen, griechische Töpferwaren, römisches Glas, ein römisches Mosaik und römische Münzen.

Um etwa 500 A.D. hatten sich die Grundformen der westlichen Zivilisation bereits gebildet und viele von ihnen bestehen heute noch.   Der letzte Teil dieses Saals befaßt sich mit dieser Dauerhaftigkeit: eine rekonstruierte Szene im modernen Basar, der Vergleich eines römischen Kochbuchs mit einem modernen und ein faszinierender Film über die Stadt Winchester, England, von ihrem keltischen Ursprung über die römische Besetzung bis in die Gegenwart.

General notes

While this assignment comes under the heading of "general" text, it must be emphasized that no text is truly "general." Every text has its own character, its own style, reason and purpose. This particular text is part of a guide to the Smithsonian Institution in Washington, DC. As such, it is written in a formal yet friendly style, conveying the cultural and historical importance of this major cultural organization in a dignified and elegant manner. The German translation seeks to preserve these qualities of the original. The difference between a mechanical, unimaginative translator, and one who goes beyond the literal sense of the words and reaches out to the spirit of the text, is the difference between "machine-like" translation and a truly human, or humanistic translation. Clearly, the goal of the serious student of translation is to become the latter, not the former.

The following examples illustrate these points.

The Smithsonian owes its origin (line 5) - This opening sentence could have read, "The Smithsonian was started by," or "built as a result of a bequest by." "Owes its origin," however, is much more elegant and dignified, and the German translation sought to preserve this sense by rendering it *verdankt ihre Entstehung*.

"The Establishment," (line 15) - This term remains untranslated in German, since it is a legal entity, and also because it would lose its meaning in translation. One could also argue for adding an equivalent German term **in brackets** following these words.

Chief Justice (line 17) - Legal and political titles vary from country to country. One should take great care in rendering such titles, so as not to confuse the meaning. A short trip to the reference sources can be very salubrious.

6 percent (line 22) - Percent can also be spelled "per cent," or rendered by the symbol %. Whichever way you go, stick to it, and don't change the designation in midstream.

The Castle (page 56, line 6) - Here *Das Schloß* was chosen over, say, *Die Burg*, since the latter is a fortified structure, built to withstand a siege, while the former is a chateau, not built or equipped for battle.

Grace Church and Saint Patrick's Cathedral (line 10) - Grace remains untranslated, while St. Patrick is preceded by *Kathedrale*, which is the German language sequence, rather than St. Patricks Kathedrale, which is an Anglicism.

10,000 years ago (line 22) - The comma in English numbers over 1000 is replaced by a period in German.

Die vorstehenden Vorschriften und die anderen Bestimmungen dieses Vertrages, die sich auf die Führung der Kapitalkonten beziehen, sind entsprechend den Durchführungsbestimmungen des Paragraphen 1.704-1(b) auszulegen und entsprechend den Durchführungsbestimmungen anzuwenden. In dem Fall, daß der Komplementär bestimmt, daß es angebracht ist, die Berechnung der Kapitalkonten oder der Belastungen und Gutschriften der Kapitalkonten zu ändern, um den Durchführungsbestimmungen zu entsprechen, so kann der Komplementär die Änderungen vornehmen vorausgesetzt, daß diese keine materiellen Auswirkungen auf die Beträge haben, die an die Gesellschafter oder Anteilsinhaber gemäß Paragraph 8 dieses Vertrages bei Auflösung der Gesellschaft zu verteilen sind.

1.10 **"Kapitaleinlage"** in bezug auf den Komplementär oder Anteilsinhaber, einschließlich aller Kommanditisten, umfaßt alle Bareinlagen (seien es entweder die ursprünglichen oder sonstige Einlagen), die von dem Anteilsinhaber und Rechtsvorgängern von Anteilsinhabern zu dem Kapital der Gesellschaft geleistet worden sind. Zur Kapitaleinlage gehört auch der ursprüngliche Bruttowert von Vermögensgegenständen, die der Gesellschafter eingebracht hat.

1.11 **"Kapitalgeschäft"** bedeutet ein zwischenzeitliches Kapitalgeschäft und/oder ein abschließendes Kapitalgeschäft.

1.12 **"Cash Flow"** bedeutet Barmittel aus allen Quellen (ausschließlich Kapitaleinlagen, Darlehenserträge und zwischenzeitliche und abschließende Kapitalgeschäfte) ohne Abzüge für Abschreibung oder Amortisation, aber nach Abzug von Barmitteln, die für die Begleichung aller anderen Ausgaben, Tilgungen, Kapitalinvestitionen und Wiederbeschaffungen aufgewendet und für den Aufbau und die Wiederaufstockung von Reserven verwendet werden.

1.13 **"Gesetz"** bedeutet der Internal Revenue Code (amerikanisches Einkommensteuergesetz) aus dem Jahre 1986 einschließlich nachfolgender Änderungen (oder entsprechende Bestimmungen in einem späteren Gesetz).

1.14 **"Kommission"** bedeutet die Securities und Exchange Commission (amerikanisches Börsenaufsichtsamt).

1.15 **"Abschreibung"** bedeutet für jedes Geschäftsjahr oder sonstigen Zeitraum einen Betrag, der der Abschreibung, Amortisation oder dem sonstigen Abzug für Kostenerstattungen entspricht, die für einen Vermögenswert für das Jahr oder sonstigen Zeitraum erlaubt ist, außer wenn der Bruttowert eines Vermögenswertes zu Beginn des Jahres oder einem sonstigen Zeitpunkt von dem Wert seiner berichtigten Besteuerungsgrundlage für Bundeseinkommensteuern abweicht. Die Abschreibung ist ein Betrag, der im selben Verhältnis zu dem anfänglichen Bruttowert des Vermögensgegenstandes steht wie die Abschreibung, Amortisation oder der sonstige Abzug für Kostenerstattungen für das Jahr oder anderen Zeitraum zu der anfänglichen Besteuerungsgrundlage steht; vorausgesetzt jedoch, daß, wenn die Abschreibung, Amortisation oder der sonstige Abzug für Kostenerstattungen für das Jahr null beträgt, die Abschreibung in bezug auf den anfänglichen Bruttowert des Vermögensgegenstandes aufgrund einer angemessenen Methode, die von dem Komplementär gewählt wird, bestimmt wird.

1.16 "**Komplementär**" bedeutet die Person(en), die als "Komplementär" im Unterschriftsblock am Ende dieses Vertrages aufgeführt ist/sind oder ein Unternehmen oder eine juristische Person, die aus denselben Personen und Ersatzpersonen besteht, die in diesem Vertrag vorgesehen sind. Der/die genannte(n) Komplementär(e) kann/können nach eigenem Ermessen und ohne Zustimmung der Kommanditisten weitere Komplementäre aufnehmen oder Personen als Komplementäre entfernen (ohne daß dies die Anteile, Aufgaben und Pflichten des/der Komplementär(s)(e) beeinträchtigt).

1.17 "**Bruttovermögenswert**" bedeutet in bezug auf alle Vermögenswerte, laut Bestimmung durch den einbringenden Gesellschafter und der Gesellschaft:

1.17.1 Der ursprüngliche Bruttowert aller Vermögenswerte, die von einem Gesellschafter in die Gesellschaft eingebracht worden sind, ist der angemessene Bruttomarktpreis des Vermögensgegenstandes, der von dem einbringenden Gesellschafter und der Gesellschaft bestimmt worden ist;

1.17.2 Der Bruttowert aller Vermögensgegenstände der Gesellschaft wird zu den folgenden Zeitpunkten an die entsprechenden angemessenen Bruttomarktpreise, die vom Komplementär bestimmt worden sind, angeglichen: **(a)** zum Zeitpunkt des Erwerbs eines zusätzlichen Gesellschaftsanteils durch einen neuen oder bestehenden Gesellschafter gegen eine Kapitaleinlage, die eine mehr als *de minimis* Einlage darstellt; **(b)** zum Zeitpunkt der Ausschüttung durch die Gesellschaft an einen Gesellschafter oder Anteilsinhaber von Anteilen, die einen mehr als *de minimis* Betrag des Gesellschaftsvermögens darstellen und **(c)** zum Zeitpunkt der Liquidation der Gesellschaft gemäß Paragraph 1.704-1(b)(2)(ii)(g) der Durchführungsbestimmungen; vorausgesetzt, daß die Berichtigungen gemäß (a) und (b) nur dann vorgenommen werden, wenn der Komplementär berechtigterweise bestimmt, daß solche Berichtigungen notwendig oder angemessen sind, um den verhältnismäßigen wirtschaftlichen Interessen der Gesellschafter und Anteilsinhaber zu entsprechen;

1.17.3 Der Bruttovermögenswert eines Gesellschaftsvermögensgegenstandes, der an einen Gesellschafter oder Anteilsinhaber ausgeschüttet wird, entspricht dem angemessenen Bruttomarktpreis des Vermögensgegenstandes am Tag der Ausschüttung; und

1.17.4 Der Bruttowert von Gesellschaftsvermögensgegenständen wird erhöht (oder vermindert) um alle Berichtigungen der berichtigten Besteuerungsgrundlage dieser Vermögenswerte gemäß Paragraph 734(b) oder Paragraph 743(b) des Gesetzes zu reflektieren, aber nur soweit, wie solche Berichtigungen bei der Feststellung der Kapitalkonten gemäß den Durchführungsbestimmungen des Paragraphen 1.704-1(b)(2)(iv)(m) berücksichtigt werden.

Falls der Bruttowert eines Vermögensgegenstandes gemäß diesem Paragraphen festgesetzt oder berichtigt worden ist, so wird der Bruttowert des Vermögensgegenstandes danach durch die Abschreibung, die bei der Gewinn- und Verlustberechnung für den Gegenstand benutzt worden ist, berichtigt.

1.18   "**Anteilsinhaber**" sind die natürlichen oder juristischen Personen, die von Zeit zu Zeit in den Büchern und Unterlagen der Gesellschaft als Anteilseigentümer eingetragen sind unabhängig davon, ob solche natürlichen oder juristischen Personen als Kommanditisten in die Gesellschaft aufgenommen worden sind.

1.19   "**Zwischenzeitliche Kapitalgeschäfte**" bedeutet die folgenden Ereignisse: (i) den Verkauf eines Teils des Immobilie; (ii) Erhalt von Versicherungsbeträgen oder sonstigen Schadenersatzzahlungen durch die Gesellschaft in bezug auf Verluste, die Wiederherstellungskosten übersteigen; (iii) Erhalt von Enteignungszahlungen für einen Teil der Immobilie und (iv) die Refinanzierung von Darlehen an die Gesellschaft oder der ursprüngliche Erhalt von Finanzierung in dem Umfang, in dem die Erträge nicht für Ausgaben verwendet werden, die durch Reparaturen oder die Wiederherstellung der Immobilie entstanden sind, oder die für die Zahlung von Verbindlichkeiten, die durch den Erwerb, die Bebauung oder die Unterhaltung der Immobilie entstehen, für sie zurückgestellt oder verwendet worden sind.

1.20   "**Grundstück**" umfaßt alle Immobilien, die die Gesellschaft zu irgendeinem Zeitpunkt besitzt.

General comments:

a. *Subject matter*

This text represents a specific area of law, namely, business or industrial law as it applies to a business agreement or contract. With this in mind, one should be sensitive to the requirements of legal translation, which means careful attention not only to the text but all the small details that go along with it, as will be explained in the examples below. Here a good English-German legal dictionary would be most useful.

b. *Format*

We draw your attention to the fact that the original text is typed in a legal text format, following established form. Therefore, the German translation was formatted to look like the original, and each page of translation corresponds exactly to each page of the original. This was done for several good reasons: (a) an end-user of a translation would often need to compare the two texts, and this exact replication makes it very easy to compare, and also to make sure nothing is missing; (b) it helps the translator to check his/her own work, making sure nothing was left out; and (c) it conveys the sense of orderliness and accuracy which is critical in legal documents.

Capital Accounts (line 6) - This document contains both banking and legal terminology, which require knowledge and reference sources for both. One cannot properly handle this kind of terminology purely on a "descriptive " basis, but must know the exact usage in both English and German.

General Partner (lines 7-8) - Again, a legal term which must be specific, and which is also capitalized as a legal term.

"Cash Flow" (line 23) - Left untranslated in the German. Some English financial terms have found their way into other languages, and are repeated unchanged.

"Code" (line 28) - This term, on the other hand, is translated, since it is a common word with good equivalents in other languages.

de minimis (page 58, line 18) - The Latin term is kept untranslated in German, since it is a term understood and used on both sides of the Atlantic.

Additional observations:

Since legal documents such as business agreements contain a fairly standard text, you may want to get hold of one or more texts of such German-language agreements, to familiarize yourself with the style and terminology. Clearly, one does not always have the time and means to obtain this kind of information, but if this is a subject you expect to translate fairly regularly, it is worth the effort.

Also, it is important to know the purpose of a particular translation, although a translator is not always given this information by the client. If it is to be used as a legally binding agreement, it has to be accurate to the point of being accepted as a legal contract. On the other hand, if it is only for information purposes - say the end-user in this case does not read English - then you need not spend nearly as much time and effort to make sure every single word is the best possible equivalent of the original.

Diskussion

Ziel unserer Umfrage war es, zum einen den Umfang der verschiedenen Knochentransplantationen, insbesondere der allogenen Transplantationen in der Bundesrepublik Deutschland zu erfassen, zum zweiten die Unterschiede in der Knochenbanklogistik aufzuzeigen. Die Auswahlkriterien der Kliniken richteten sich nach der Größe und dem Aufgabengebiet. Da die Knochenbanktechnik mit einem nicht unerheblichen technischen, materiellen und personellen Aufwand verbunden ist, wurden von vornherein Krankenhäuser mit weniger als 60 chirurgischen Betten bzw. Kliniken, die nach Angaben in "Deutsche Chirurgie '88" [13] keine Unfallchirurgie durchführen, nicht angeschrieben.

Der hohe Rücklauf der Fragebögen mit 46,4% läßt den Schluß zu, daß die Fragestellung des Erhebungsbogens als sinnvoll akzeptiert wurde. Immerhin konnten chirurgische Kliniken mit insgesamt ca. 39 000 Betten erfaßt werden.

Tabelle 2. Untersuchungen des Knochenspenders vor der allogenen
Transplantation an 209 Kliniken

	ja		nein	
	n	%	n	%
Hepatitis B	184	88	21	10
HIV	174	83	31	15
Lues	162	78	43	21
Bakteriologie qual.	155	74	50	24
Rhesus-Faktor	61	29	134	64
Histoloie	48	23	157	75
Blutgruppen	45	22	152	73
Bakteriologie quant.	45	22	160	77
Bakteriologie als Zwischenanalyse	26	12	179	86
Cytomegalie	12	6	193	92
Malaria	1	0.5	204	98

Interessant ist bereits das Verhältnis der Kliniken, die keine, nur autogene oder autogene und allogene Knochentransplantationen durchführen. Lediglich 5% der Kliniken führten keine Knochentransplantationen durch. 39% gewannen ihre Transplantate als autogene und 45%

verwendeten u.a. auch allogene Knochentransplantate. Demnach wurde im Erhebungsjahr 1987 in 209 Kliniken über 6000mal allogener Knochen transplantiert.

Unter Berücksichtigung, daß etwa die Hälfte der Kliniken nicht geantwortet hatte und die orthopädischen Kliniken nicht angeschrieben wurden (21 500 Betten nach Angaben des Statistischen Bundesamtes in Wiesbaden von 1987), erscheint eine Schätzung von jährlich ca. 15 000 allogenen Knochentransplantationen in der Bundesrepublik Deutschland durchaus gerechtfertigt. Trotz dieser hohen Zahl durchgeführter Transplantationen ist aus den Ergebnissen der Erhebungsbögen kein einheitliches Konzept in der Knochenbanktechnik erkennbar. Aus den Ergebnissen seien daher nur einige Zahlen kommentiert, wobei die Varianz der Ergebnisse für sich spricht.

Bei den Spenderuntersuchungen fällt auf, daß die serologischen Tests auf übertragbare Viruserkrankungen und die bakteriellen Untersuchungen in ca. 25% der Kliniken nicht durchgeführt wurden. Nachdem eindeutig nachgewiesen ist, daß kältekonservierter allogener Knochen bakterielle wie virale Krankheiten, insbesondere auch HIV übertragen kann [6, 10], ist die Unterlassung dieser Untersuchungen sowohl medizinisch wie juristisch nicht vertretbar.

Die Blutgruppen wurden in 73%, die Rhesus-Faktoren in 64% nicht beachtet. Dies ist um so bedenklicher, da zumindest für die Rhesus-Faktoren einzelne Kausalitäten über die Antikörperbildung nach rhesusinkompatibel durchgeführten Knochentransplantationen bei jüngeren Frauen vorliegen [9, 10, 12]. In eigenen Untersuchungen können wir außerdem nachweisen, daß auch im ABO-System Antikörper nach inkompatibel transplantiertem Knochen beim Empfänger gebildet werden. Dies kann bei Frauen während einer Schwangerschaft zur Ausbildung eines Morbus haemolyticus neonatorum führen [11]. Die Richtlinien des wissenschaftlichen Beirates der Bundesärztekammer schreiben bisher keine zwingende Beachtung des Rhesus-Systems bzw. der ABO-Blutgruppen vor [17].

Bei der Transplantatbehandlung, Verpackung und Lagerung zeigen sich ebenfalls erhebliche Unterschiede. Von der Verpackung ist zu fordern, daß diese sicher vor einer sekundären Kontamination schützen muß. Dies ist durch eine leicht zu beschädigende Einfachverpackung in Plastiktüten nicht gewährleistet.

Offenbar bestehen auch über die Indikationen zum Zusatz lokaler Antibiotika oder Desinfektionsmittel zum allogenen Transplantat erhebliche Unterschiede. Während 72 Kliniken eine lokale adjuvante Antibiotika-Therapie durchführen, wird diese von der Mehrzahl der Kliniken nicht angewendet.

Die Lagerungstemperatur und Lagerungsdauer sowie Verpackungsart sind Indikatoren dafür, inwieweit der allogene Knochen entsprechend den Anforderungen an ein biologisches Transplantat eingeordnet wird. Eine Einfachverpackung bei einer Lagerungstemperatur von -18°C kann den Anforderungen eines biologischen Transplantates nicht angemessen sein [3,15]. Auch eine maximale Lagerungsdauer von bis zu 5 Jahren erscheint hinsichtlich der biologischen Qualität des Transplantates sowie möglicher bakterieller Kontaminationen als bedenklich [3].

Die AIDS-Problematik führte bei einigen Kliniken zur Aufgabe der allogenen Knochentransplantationen. Bei anderen Kliniken hat sie offenbar nicht einmal zur Durchführung der HIV-Serologie Anlaß gegeben. Auch die inzwischen obligat vorgeschriebene schriftliche Einverständniserklärung beim Spender sowie die zweite HIV-Testung wurden nur selten durchgeführt. Von der Wahrscheinlichkeit, mit der allogenen Knochentransplantation eine Infektionskrankheit zu übertragen, stehen sicher die Hepatitis und bakteriellen Krankheiten vor der HIV-Infektion. Daher erscheint es mindestens ebenso bedenklich, daß diese viel häufigeren Krankheiten in 10-24% der Fälle beim Spender nicht ausgeschlossen wurden und somit auf den Empfänger übertragen werden können.

Auch die Möglichkeit der Übertragung tumoröser Erkrankungen scheint in der Führung der Knochenbanktechniken bei vielen Kliniken keine Beachtung zu finden, da 75% keine histologischen Untersuchungen der Transplantate durchführen.

Die Ergebnisse der Umfrage bestätigen, daß trotz einer Fülle von Publikationen über allogene Knochentransplantationen bzw. Knochenbanksysteme in der Bundesrepublik Deutschland ein breites Spektrum unterschiedlicher Knochenbanktechniken vorherrscht, die teilweise mit neueren Erkenntnissen und Empfehlungen nicht mehr vereinbar sind. Von einer Standardisierung kann keinesfalls gesprochen werden. Die allogene Knochentransplantation ist wie eine Organtransplantation aufzufassen und muß unter entsprechend strengen Kriterien hinsichtlich der Spender- und Empfängerauswahl sowie der Transplantatlagerung erfolgen. Aus medizinischen wie juristischen Erwägungen ist von daher ein einheitliches Management in der Knochenbanktechnik unerläßlich.

Wir danken allen Kliniken, die sich aktiv an unserer Umfrage beteiligt haben, für ihre Mitarbeit.

General comments:

This is a scientific medical paper which requires not only direct translation into German, but also a careful revision of one's translation to achieve good German readability, in view of the length and complexity of many of the sentences. The following examples show some of the pitfalls of the material, and you may want to check and see how they match your own "rough spots" in doing this particular assignment. A good English-German chemical dictionary would certainly be very helpful, but one also needs a general understanding of the subject matter and a familiarity with this kind of writing.

allogeneic (line 8) - When in doubt about any spelling of medical terminology, do not hesitate to look it up. Misspellings of medical text can be both embarrassing and costly.

46.4% (line 15) - The English decimal period becomes a comma in German.

39,000 (line 17) - The comma in English in numbers over 1000 becomes either a period or a space in German. Whichever you use, stick to it and do not change it in midstream

Table 2. (table) - Table, charts, graphs etc. are very common in technical documents. With the new computer graphics and word processings wonders, you can reproduce such items to look almost identical to the original. Such work, which used to be very time-consuming and technically difficult only a few years ago, is now quite easy, and expected of the freelance translator.
(Note: The number of clinics in the table adds up to 205, **not** 209 as stated in the heading. In this case, the translator must adhere to the original figure, with the option of adding "[sic]" after 209 or appending a "Translator's Note" on a separate page.)

The ratio of the clinics... (line 21) - This sentence is somewhat ambiguous, and requires careful reading and correction.

HIV (page 61, line 15) - This English acronym remains untranslated in German.

AIDS (line 42) - See "HIV" above.

DIE NOTWENDIGKEIT NEUER ANSÄTZE. Im kommenden Jahrzehnt wird sich die Nachfrage nach Infrastrukturinvestitionen in zwei unterschiedlichen Länderkategorien gleichermaßen erhöhen: zum einen in Ländern, die eine gesamtwirtschaftliche Anpassung mit konsequent niedrigen Investionsniveaus ertragen haben, und zum anderen in solchen Ländern, in denen ein starkes Wachstum die bestehende Infrastruktur nun erheblich belastet. Infrastrukturinvestitionen in Entwicklungsländern machen im Durchschnitt 4 Prozent des BIP aus -- sie müßten aber oft beträchtlich höher sein. In Fällen, in denen der Telekommunikationsbereich oder die Energieversorgungsnetze rasch expandieren, können die jährlichen Investitionen im jeweiligen Sektor durchaus 2 Prozent des BIP erreichen. Ein die Investitionsnachfrage belebender Sonderfaktor ist in vielen Ländern die rasche Zunahme der Verstädterung, wodurch Investitionen in die Wasserversorgung, die Müllbehandlung und -beseitigung notwendig werden.

Für Asien wird geschätzt, daß sich der Anteil der Infrastrukturinvestitionen am BIP von gegenwärtig 4 Prozent bis zur Jahrtausendwende auf über 7 Prozent steigert; hierbei dürften das Transportwesen und der Energiesektor voraussichtlich den Großteil der Ressourcen beanspruchen, gefolgt von der Telekommunikation und der Umweltinfrastruktur. Einige der geplanten Investitionen sind beispiellos. So hat sich zum Beispiel China das Ziel gesetzt, bis 1995 jährlich zumindest 5 Millionen Telefonanschlüsse zu installieren und in den Folgejahren zumindest 8 Million; damit soll sich der 1992 vorhandene Bestand von 18 Millionen Anschlüssen bis zum Jahr 2000 mehr als verdreifachen.

Privates Unternehmertum: Tendenzen und Chancen

Die gegenwärtigen Bemühungen um eine größere Unterstützung und Risikoübernahme der Privaten bei Infrastrukturprojekten spiegeln diese verschiedenen Herausforderungen wider. Nach Jahrzehnten erheblicher regulativer Einschränkungen hat gegen Ende der achtziger Jahre das private Unternehmertum im Bereich der Infrastruktur neues Gewicht erlangt, und zwar auf zweierlei Weise: erstens infolge der Privatisierung staatseigener Versorgungsbetriebe und zweitens durch Reformen des regulativen Rahmens, die es ermöglichten, daß neue Einrichtungen im Wettbewerb mit bestehenden Betrieben -- oder komplementär zu ihnen -- errichtet werden konnten.

Die bedeutendsten neuen Privatanbieter im Bereich der Infrastruktur sind internationale Unternehmen, die in Entwicklungsländern Geschäftsmöglichkeiten suchen und oft in Zusammenarbeit mit örtlichen Gesellschaften operieren. Diese Unternehmen bringen nicht nur ihre Managementerfahrungen und technischen Fertigkeiten ein, sondern auch ihre Kreditwürdigkeit und ihre Fähigkeit, Investitionen in Entwicklungsländern finanzieren zu können. Bedeutende Elektrizitäts-, Telekommunikations- und Wasserversorgungsbetriebe in den Industrieländern sehen sich einer nur langsam wachsenden Nachfrage und größer werdenden Wettbewerb (infolge der Deregulierung) auf ihren Heimatmärkten gegenüber. Infolgedessen suchen sie angestrengt nach hochrentablen Investitionsmöglichkeiten in Entwicklungsländern.

Baukonsortien betätigen sich im Bau von gebührenpflichtigen Straßen und der Errichtung von Energieprojekten, wobei sie sich in manchen Fällen auch am Kapital beteiligen. Einige Gesellschaften oder Gesellschaftszusammenschlüsse spezialisieren sich auch auf Einzelobjekte der Infrastruktur; sie stellen dabei Finanzierungspakete zusammen und überwachen die Projektentwicklung und den Betrieb.

Die meisten Indikatoren über Infrastrukturinvestitionen mit privater Beteiligung zeigen ein rasches Wachstum. Privatisierte Telekommunikations- und Elektrizitätseinrichtungen in Lateinamerika und Asien tätigen große und zunehmende Neuinvestitionen. Die Anzahl dieser sogenannten Projekte "auf der grünen Wiese" - insbesondere im Straßenbau und im Bereich der Stromversorgung - ist stark gewachsen (wie weiter unten dargelegt wird). Die Infrastrukturinvestitionen der internationalen Finanzkorporation (International Finance Corporation - IFC), eine Tochtergesellschaft der Weltbank, die ausschließlich in Privatobjekte investiert, haben stark zugenommen, und zwar von bescheidenen Beträgen gegen Ende der achtziger Jahre auf 330 Mio Dollar im Fiskaljahr 1993. Der von der IFC investierte Betrag zog zehnmal höhere Fremdmittel nach sich, so daß die IFC 1993 an privaten Investitionen in Höhe von 3,5 Mrd Dollar partizipierte.

Die wichtigste Entwicklung während der letzten vier Jahre lag in der explosiven Zunahme ausländischer, langfristiger Mittelzuflüsse privater Geldgeber in die Entwicklungsländer -- insbesondere in Form von ausländischen Direkt- und Portfolioinvestitionen. Im Jahr 1992 beliefen sich diese Kapitalströme insgesamt auf mehr als 80 Mrd Dollar, und es wird für das Jahr 1993 ein Anstieg auf 112 Mrd Dollar erwartet (Tabelle 5.1). Der Infrastrukturbereich war ein bedeutender Empfänger solcher Mittel (Sonderbeitrag 5.2).

Die Privatinvestitionen in der Entwicklung der Infrastruktur belaufen sich gegenwärtig auf insgesamt 15 Mrd Dollar pro Jahr oder auf 7 Prozent der jährlich 200 Mrd Dollar, die in Entwicklungsländern für die Infrastruktur ausgegeben werden. Der Anteil privater Investitionen im Bereich der Infrastruktur ist zwar gering, gleichwohl aber erheblich höher als noch vor wenigen Jahren, und die Wahrscheinlichkeit ist groß, daß die Privatinvestitionen weiter wachsen werden, womit sich ihr Anteil am Gesamtvolumen bis zum Jahr 2000 verdoppeln könnte. Ein Anzeichen hierfür ist das sich gegenwärtig bei der IFC in Vorbereitung befindliche Investitionsvolumen, das fast so hoch ist wie der gesamte bislang finanzierte Projektbestand.

Der geringe Gesamtanteil privater Finanzierungen im Bereich der Infrastruktur verdeckt große regionale und sektorale Unterschiede. Die Privatfinanzierung spielt in Lateinamerika eine viel größere Rolle als in anderen Teilen der Welt und hat in den Bereichen Telekommunikation und Stromerzeugung einen größeren Umfang als in anderen Sektoren. Die Ausbreitung der aktuellen Erfahrungen auf alle Regionen und Sektoren wird zu einem steigenden Anteil privater Engagements und Finanzierungen, gemessen am Gesamtvolumen, führen. So werden zum Beispiel die Privatisierung im Telekommunikationsbereich und eine unabhängige Energieerzeugung in allen Regionen der Welt erörtert, auch in Afrika südlich der Sahara, und stetige technische und finanzielle Innovationen werden ohne Zweifel eine private Finanzierung attraktiver machen. So könnten zum Beispiel elektronische Methoden zur Identifizierung von Fahrzeugen und zur Erhebung von Straßenbenutzungsgebühren dazu führen, daß das Straßennetz mehr einem öffentlichen Versorgungsbetrieb ähnelt, womit auch der Anteil privater

Finanzierungen des Fernstraßennetzes in die Höhe schnellen könnte.

Selbst bei einem ansteigenden Anteil privat finanzierter Infrastruktureinrichtungen wird der Staat auch weiterhin eine wichtige Finanzierungsquelle bleiben. Oft wird er Partner privater Unternehmer sein müssen. Eine Partnerschaft zwischen öffentlicher Hand und privatem Sektor bedeutet in mancher Hinsicht eine Rückkehr ins neunzehnte Jahrhundert, als in großen Teilen der Welt Infrastrukturprojekte privat finanziert wurden, während gleichzeitig die staatliche Unterstützung stimulierend wirkte. Von den Erfahrungen während des neunzehnten Jahrhunderts gehen aber auch wichtige Warnsignale aus (Sonderbeitrag 5.3).

Tabelle 5.1 Ausländische Portfolio- und Direktinvestitionen in Entwicklungsländern, 1990 bis 1993

(Nettozuflüsse in Mrd US-Dollar)

Art	1990	1991	1992	1993[a]
Ausländische Aktienkäufe˙	3,78	7,55	13,07	13,1
Geschlossene Investmentfonds[b]	2,78	1,20	1,34	2,7
ADRs und GDRs[c]	0,14	4,90	5,93	7,2
Direkte Aktienkäufe	0,77	1,45	5,80	3,2
Schuldeninstrumente	5,56	12,72	23,73	42,6
Anleihen	4,68	10,19	21,24	39,1
Wechsel	0,23	1,38	0,85	1,6
Einlagenzertifikate	0,65	1,15	1,64	1,8
Gesamte Portfolioinvestitionen[d]	9,34	20,27	36,80	55,7
Ausländische Direktinvestitionen	26,30	36,90	47,30	56,3
Insgesamt	35,64	57,17	84,10	112,0

Anmerkung: Diese Tabelle enthält alle Portfolio- und Direktinvestitionsströme. Separate Angaben für die Infrastruktur stehen nicht zur Verfügung.

a. Die Angaben für 1993 sind Schätzungen oder Projektionen.

b. Ein geschlossener Investmentfonds verfügt über einen beschränkten Umfang der auszugebenden Anteile und in manchen Fällen auch über einen festgelegten Anlagezeitraum.

c. ADR = American depository receipts (Amerikanisches Hinterlegungszertifikat); GDR = global depository receipts (Globales Hinterlegungszertifikat). Ein ADR ist ein Instrument, das von einer Offshore-Gesellschaft zur Eigenkapitalaufnahme in den Vereinigten Staaten genutzt wird, ohne formelle Notierung an einer amerikanischen Aktienbörse. Bei GDRs handelt es sich um ähnliche Instrumente, die in Europa und anderswo eingesetzt werden.

d. Portfolioinvestitionen errechnen sich als Summe der Käufe von Aktien und Schuldeninstrumenten.

Quelle: Weltbank (1993i), S. 10, 21.

General comments:

a Financial Translation

In translation, there is a basic difference between translating financial subjects and other technical subjects, such as legal or medical. While it is relatively easy to master the methodology of working with most technical vocabularies even if one does not have the technical or professional background of the particular field in which one translates, in financial subjects it is necessary to have at least a general knowledge of the subject. This may be due to the fact that financial terminology and concepts are not always as readily translatable as as other technical subjects. The upshot of all this is that one should not be hasty to accept a financial translation assignment if one does not work in this field on a regular basis.

b. Subject matter

This particular assignment consists of a text derived from a publication of an international financial organization. As with most major organizations and corporations, this organization has its own so-called "corporate style," which affects the way this material is translated. Normally, an organization of this magnitude employs its own translators, or uses outside translators on a regular basis, to acquaint them with its style. If called upon to translate this kind of text, be sure to familiarize yourself with the organization's style.

GDP (line 9) - Becomes BIP in German (gross domestic product). Acronyms can be a major headaches for translators, and acquiring as well as self-developing good glossaries in this field is a critical function of technical translation.

7 percent (line 16) - Whether you use the word or the symbol for percentage, be consistent and use the same item throughout.

International Finance Corporation (IFC) (page 64, line 3) - Here the name of the organization is translated into German, but IFC remains unchanged. This is an example of an acronym which may not be universally familiar.

$330 million (line 5) - In German the U.S. currency is spelled out rather than indicated by its symbol.

$3.5 billion (line 6) - The period becomes a comma in German.

Additional notes:

The table at the end of this assignment consists of technical financial language. Here thorough familiarity with this kind of terminology, and with the institution that generates such terminology is critical. In undertaking this kind of translation, one should have a good line of communication with the organization that generates this text, to be sure the client and the translator are on the same wavelength.

SECTION 3

WHERE DO WE GO FROM HERE?

After you have completed all the assignments, or at least those you have chosen to do, you have to make a major decision. If you have never translated for profit before, you have to ask yourself if you are ready to try your hand at soliciting for-profit translation work. If the answer is yes, turn to the book in this Kit, *Guide for Translators,* and read Chapters 9 and 10, on how to operate successfully as a freelance translator, and where to find work. If you have translated for profit before in a specific area, such as legal documents, and you feel you are now ready to venture into another area, such as medical translation, first try out some short assignments in that field, until you become comfortable with it.

In either case, the next step is to turn to Appendix 3 in the book, and look up sources of translation work. We urge you to develop a relationship with one or more translation companies in your own geographical area. There is absolutely no reason in this day and age for a translator, say, in Wisconsin, not to develop a profitable relationship with a translation company in Florida, and in time you may indeed find out that a certain company on the other side of the continent is your best source of work. But as a beginner, there are many advantages to interfacing personally with the staff of a translation company close to home. They can give you a great deal of practical advice, help you with the hardware and the software, and share other kinds of experience with you. There is an old saying: A good neighbor is better than a distant relative.

If, on the other hand, you feel you are not ready to take the plunge, you may want to consider a translation course or study program. Refer to Appendix 4 in the book, and see if there is a program close to home you can sign up for. Or you may decide to continue practicing on your own.

Whatever you decide to do, don't give up too easily. If you do enjoy the challenge of translation, continue to improve you skills. Remember: Translation can be a full-time career or a very fulfilling and profitable sideline. It is definitely the kind of expertise worth having, no matter what else you choose to do with your time.

APPENDIX A: REQUISITES FOR PROFESSIONAL TRANSLATORS

Any person who knows more than one language has the ability to explain a word or a sentence in what translators call "the source language" (the language you translate from) by using an equivalent word or sentence in what they call "the target language" (the language you translate into). This, in effect, is the beginning of translation. But it is only the beginning. It does not automatically turn a person into an accomplished translator. Along with the knowledge of the source and the target language, a translator must have an aptitude for translation. Some people are endowed with a talent for translation. It is not an acquired skill, like riding a bicycle. It is rather a talent, like playing the violin. Some people have it and some don't. It is not necessarily an indication of a lower or higher IQ. Nor is it an indication of how linguistically gifted one is. It is an inborn skill that enables a person to change a text from one language into another quickly and accurately, or, if you will, think in more than one language at the same time. If you possess this skill, then it behooves you to develop it and make use of it, because there is never an overabundance of good translators, and it is almost axiomatic that the good ones can always find either full-time or part-time work.

The **first** requisite for the working translator is a thorough knowledge of both the source and the target languages. There is no point in billing oneself as a translator if one is not fully familiar with both languages, or does not possess a vocabulary in both equal to that of a speaker of those languages who has a university education or its equivalent.

The **second** requisite is thorough "at-homeness" in both cultures. A language is a living phenomenon. It does not exist apart from the culture where it is spoken and written. It communicates not only the names of objects and different kinds of action, but also feelings, attitudes, beliefs, and so on. To be fully familiar with a language, one must also be familiar with the culture in which the language is used, indeed, with the people who use it, their ways, manners, beliefs and all that goes into making a culture.

Third, one must keep up with the growth and change of the language, and be up-to-date in all of its nuances and neologisms. Languages are in a constant state of flux, and words change meaning from year to year. A pejorative term can become laudatory, and a neutral term can become loaded with meaning. Thirty years ago the English word "gay" simply meant "joyous." Now it is used to define an entire segment of society. We once spoke of the "almighty dollar." Now as we travel abroad we may find out the dollar is not necessarily everyone's preferred currency.

Fourth, a distinction must be made between the languages one translates from and into. Generally speaking, one translates from another language into one's own native language. This is because one is usually intimately familiar with one's own language, while even years of study and experience do not necessarily enable one to be completely at home with an acquired language. The exceptions to this rule are usually those people who have lived in more than one culture, and have spoken more than one language on a regular basis. Those may be able to translate in both directions. There are also rare gifted individuals who have mastered another language to such a degree that they can go both ways. They are indeed extremely rare. Given all of this, one should allow for the fact that while the ability of the accomplished translator to write and speak in the target language (i.e., one's native tongue) may be flawless, that person may not necessarily be able to write excellent prose or give great speeches in the source language (i.e., the language from which one translates). Then again, it is not necessary to be able to write and speak well in the language one translates from, while it is to be expected that a good translator is also a good writer and speaker in his or her native language.

Fifth, a professional translator has to be able to translate in more than one area of knowledge. Most professional translators are called upon to translate in a variety of fields. It is not uncommon for a translator to cover as many as twenty or thirty fields of knowledge in one year, including such areas as political subjects, economics, law, medicine, communications and so on. Obviously, it would be hard to find a translator who is an economist, a lawyer, a medical doctor, and an engineer all wrapped into one. In fact, such a person probably does not exist. One does not have to be a lawyer to translate legal documents. Many a professional translator has been able to gain enough knowledge and acquire a vocabulary in a variety of technical fields to be able to produce perfectly accurate and well-written translations in those fields. This is not nearly as difficult as it may seem, since most technical fields utilize a well-defined number of terms which keep repeating themselves, and as one keeps translating the same subject, they become more and more familiar to the translator. One must, however, have a natural curiosity about many different areas of human knowledge and activity, and an interest in increasing one's vocabulary in a variety of related as well as unrelated fields.

Sixth, an effective translator must have a facility for writing or speaking (depending on whether the method used is writing, speaking, or dictation), and the ability to articulate quickly and accurately, either orally or in writing. Like a reporter, a translator must be able to transmit ideas in real time, and in good understandable language. Translation is a form of writing and speech-making, and a translator is, in a sense, a writer and an orator.

Seventh, a professional translator must develop a good speed of translation. There are two reasons for this: First, most clients wait until the last minute to assign a translation job. As a result, they turn to a translator or a translation service with what is perhaps the most typical question in this business: "How soon can you have this job ready for me?" The professional translator has to be prepared to accept that long job with the short turnaround time, or there will be no repeat business from that particular client or from most other clients, for that matter. Secondly, translation is generally paid by the word. The more words one can translate per hour, the more income one will generate. Translating 50 words per hour can land a translator in the poorhouse. Serious translation starts at 250 words per hour, and can reach as high as 1000 words per hour using word processing, and close to 3000 words per hour using dictation (the author actually knows such a translator). High volume translators are the ones who will be the most successful.

Eighth, a translator must develop research skills, and be able to acquire reference sources which are essential for producing high quality translation. Without such sources even the best of translators cannot hope to be able to handle a large variety of subjects in many unrelated fields. Dedicated translators are the ones who are always on the lookout for new reference sources, and over time develop a data bank which can be used in their work.

Ninth, today's translator cannot be a stranger to hardware, software, fax, modem, the Internet, and the latest developments in all those media. Translation has become completely dependent on electronic tools. Gone are the days of handwriting, the typewriter, and all the other "prehistoric" means of communication. The more one becomes involved in translation, the more one finds oneself caught up in the latest high-tech developments.

Tenth, a translator who wishes to be busy on a fairly regular basis doing translation work must carefully consider the fact that certain languages are in high demand, say, in Washington or in Los Angeles, while others are not. Thus, for example, there is high demand for

Japanese, German, Spanish, French, Chinese, Arabic, Russian and Italian in both Washington and Los Angeles, but not nearly as much for Bulgarian, Farsi, Czech, or Afrikaans. If your language falls within the second group, it is extremely advisable to also have language expertise in one of the languages of the first group, or to seriously consider whether your particular language has enough of a demand to warrant a major investment of time and effort on your part. One should always check and see what kind of a potential one's language specialty has in a given geographic area.

The above ten points are the essential criteria for developing a translation career. There are many other considerations, but none as important as these. If you feel that you can meet all of the above criteria, then you should continue reading this handbook and putting it to good use.

The Well-Rounded Translator

The main division in the translation field is between literary and technical translation. Literary translation, which covers such areas as fiction, poetry, drama, and the humanities in general, is often done by writers of the same genre who actually author works of the same kind in the target language, or at least by translators with the required literary aptitude. For practical reasons, this handbook will not cover literary translation, but will instead focus on the other major area of translation, namely, technical translation. High quality literary translation has always been the domain of the few, and is hardly lucrative (don't even think of doing literary translation if your motive is money), while technical translation is done by a much greater number of practitioners, and is an ever-growing and expanding field with excellent earning opportunities. This chapter discusses the characteristics of the well-rounded technical translator.

The term "technical" is extremely broad. In the translation business it covers much more than technical subjects in the narrow sense of the word. In fact, there is an overlap between literary and technical translation when it comes to such areas as social sciences, political subjects, and many others.

One way of defining technical translation is by asking the question, does the subject being translated require a specialized vocabulary, or is the language non-specialized? If the text being translated includes specialized terms in a given field, then the translation is technical.

The more areas (and languages) a translator can cover, the greater the opportunity for developing a successful translation career. Furthermore, as one becomes proficient in several areas, it becomes easier to add more. Besides, many technical areas are interrelated, and proficiency in one increases proficiency in another. In addition, every area breaks down into many subareas, each with its own vocabulary and its own linguistic idiosyncrasies. Thus, for example, translating in Arabic does not make one an expert in all spoken Arabic dialects, yet a knowledge of several of those dialects is very beneficial for the professional Arabic translator.

How does one become a well-rounded translator? The answer can be summed up in one word—experience. The key to effective translation is practice. Since human knowledge grows day by day, and since language keeps growing and changing, the well-rounded translator must keep in touch with knowledge and language on a regular basis. The worst thing that can happen to a translator is to be out of touch with the source language for more than a couple of years. What the rusty translator may find out is that new words, new concepts and new ways of using those words and applying those concepts have come into being during that period of "hibernation," and one's old expertise is no longer reliable.

Translation, therefore, is a commitment one makes not for a limited period of time, but rather long-term. It is to be assumed that anyone who becomes a translator is the kind of person who loves words and loves the challenge of using words effectively and correctly. Such a person will not become an occasional translator, but will make translation a lifelong practice.

Good and Bad Translation Habits

The accomplished translator can develop good as well as bad habits. Starting with the bad, we have already pointed out one—losing touch with the source language for long periods of time. Another bad habit is taking illegitimate shortcuts while translating. There are several types of such shortcuts. The most typical is failing to look up a word one is really not sure how to translate. Being ninety percent sure of a word's meaning is not good enough in professional translation. If one is not sure of a word's meaning, even after all available means have been exhausted, then one must put in a translator's note to that effect, or make it known in some other way that there is a problem with translating that particular word. Anything less would be deceptive.

Another illegitimate shortcut is summarizing a paragraph instead of providing a *full* translation. There is such a thing as summary translation of a paragraph or a document. If a summary is called for, then this is precisely what the translator is expected to provide. But the most common form of translation is what's known in the business as a verbatim translation, which is a full and complete rendition of the source text. When verbatim translation is ordered, anything less than a full translation is an illegitimate shortcut. Unfortunately, some translators tend to overlook this from time to time, especially when they undertake more work than they can accomplish by a given deadline, and decide to summarize rather than miss that deadline.

Perhaps the worst habit for a translator is to decide at a certain point in time that his or her knowledge of either the source or the target language is so good that it cannot possibly stand any improvement. The moment one stops growing linguistically, one is no longer on the cutting edge of one's profession. The good translator is a perennial language student, always eager and willing to learn more and to keep up with the latest.

As for good habits, the most important, perhaps, are the ones we obtain by reversing the above-mentioned bad habits. But there are many more. One excellent habit is to read professional literature in the field one will be called upon to translate in with reasonable frequency. One good example is *Scientific American*, which can help anyone who translates subjects of science and technology to learn the style or styles used in scientific writing. People who work in the field of translating business documents should definitely read business periodicals, not the least of which is *The Wall Street Journal*. One does not have to be a scientist to translate scientific articles, or have a business degree to translate business documents, but a general understanding of the subject goes a long way towards providing an accurate translation of the subject.

Another excellent habit is to translate not only for profit but also for enjoyment and experience. Most people, unfortunately, are not so taken with their daily work that they would want to continue doing it after hours for fun or practice. But an accomplished translator is someone who will on occasion translate simply for the sake of sharpening his or her skill, or accept a very small fee because of personal commitment to the subject matter, or because of a personal interest. This writer, for example, enjoys translating poetry because of the challenge of doing what is perhaps the most difficult type of translation, and, quite simply, because of the enjoyment of poetry.

Yet another good habit is always to be on the lookout for dictionaries. Many dictionaries are hard to find, and are available in few places. This writer in all his travels across the United States and abroad always stops in bookstores to look for dictionaries. One can also order dictionaries from bookstores and from publishers, but then one has to know what to order and from whom.

The last good habit I would like to mention is the practice of compiling word lists and building a reference library. Dictionaries do not have all the words and terms a translator needs, nor do they contain all the information which specialized references may have. There are aids for translators put out by certain organizations, and there is professional literature in every field. In recent years there has been a growing awareness of the need for terminology management, and with the constant advances in computer technology databases have been proliferating, making the work of the translator much easier than ever before. Good references are worth their weight in gold when they are needed for a specific translation, and over time the experienced translator develops an extensive library of glossaries which become essential for any translation assignment.

APPENDIX B: TRANSLATION TECHNIQUES

Preliminary Considerations

You are given a text to translate. Before you commit yourself to doing any work on it, you must ask yourself a few preliminary questions. They are:

1. Is the text legible?
2. Am I familiar enough with the subject to tackle it?
   Do I have the linguistic resources (dictionaries, human contacts) to decipher unfamiliar words?
4. Is the text complete, or are there any missing parts?
5. Can I do it within the requested timeframe?
6. Do I have a good reason for doing it (doing it as a learning experience, or because you enjoy it, or to help a friend, or because you are properly compensated for doing it)?

Once you have answered all the above questions to your own satisfaction, you are ready to proceed with the translation.

Effective Approaches

There is no single effective approach to translation, and over time translators develop personal techniques which enhance the quality and the speed of their translation. No one set of rules applies equally to everyone, but there are certain methods and means of translation which can help almost any translator achieve greater accuracy and output. The following is a review of some of the key techniques which are becoming almost universal among professional translators.

The first and foremost question a translator must deal with today is what kind of equipment to use in the process of translating. In the days of the pen and the typewriter this question was much less crucial. Today, however, translation has become almost totally dependent on computers, for several good reasons: (a) Word processing allows far greater flexibility in producing text than any other contemporary means. The output of most translators has been tripled and quadrupled through the use of computers; (b) Computers allow text to be stored on a disk and reprinted or modified later on, a function which is invaluable in the translation field; (c) Clients nowadays are getting used to asking for translation on disk, since it allows them to edit, reprint, modify and enhance the physical appearance of a document; (d) If more than one translator is involved in a given translation project, the text from the various translators can be entered by an editor on one disk and equalized or manipulated as necessary, without having to redo any particular portion thereof.

In addition, it is becoming more common every day to use electronic means such as a modem, fax or e-mail to transmit and receive text. These tools are no longer a luxury. Their cost has been coming down, and more and more translators are acquiring them. Many people today are saying they cannot imagine how translators were ever able to manage without them. The answer is very simple: manage we did, but it took us ten days to two weeks to do what we can now receive, translate and deliver in two or three days.

The next question when approaching a translation assignment is: Am I qualified to do this particular translation?   Only an honest answer will do.   If one is not sure, then chances are one should not tackle that particular task. One must feel confident about a particular assignment if the results are to be satisfactory. The exception to this rule is a case where a client cannot find anyone else to do that particular job, and for some good reason is either willing to take a chance or to receive less than a complete and fully accurate rendition. In such a case it should be made clear between translator and client that the translation is not legally binding.

Once the commitment is made to proceed with the job, the translator will spend some time going over the entire document – even if it is book-length – and do a realistic assessment of the following points:

a. How long will it take to translate the document?
b. What reference tools are needed to get it done?
c. What kind of preliminary steps are needed prior to the actual work of translating?
d. What special problems are related to the document, such as legibility of blurred or poorly copied
   text or difficult handwriting?
e. Does the document contain text in a language or languages other than the main source language,
   and, if so, can the translator handle that language?

Regarding the question of time, one can do a quick estimate of the length of the document by averaging words per line, times lines per page, times number of pages. An experienced translator has a pretty good idea of the number of words per hour he or she can translate. This is an essential feature of undertaking a professional translation job, since most clients have tight deadlines and tend to give repeat business to those translators known for keeping to their deadlines.

As for reference tools, if, for example, one is given a document about telecommunications, one should make use of one's own resources in that field and/or borrow from other sources whatever one needs to accomplish the task.

Preliminary steps prior to actual translation can include a consultation with an expert in a specialized technical field regarding a difficult term, phrase, paragraph or concept which the translator does not feel comfortable with. Having access to such experts is one of the translator's most cherished assets. It can make all the difference in the world between a correct and effective translation and one that misses the main point of the entire text. Another preliminary step is a trip to the local, regional or even specialized library to do some research on the subject.

The problem of legibility should be identified *before* one begins the task, not after. Sometimes the problem may start in the middle of the document and be so severe as to render the translation of the first part useless. In that case, the translator may have wasted a great deal of time. Sometimes the problem is minor, and does not affect the overall outcome of the translation. In other cases, the client may decide to proceed with the translation and simply put the designation [illegible] (between brackets rather than parentheses) wherever a word or part of the text cannot be deciphered.

Unbeknownst to client and translator, when a translation job is first assigned, there may be portions of text inside the source document in a language other than the main language of the document. This can happen in commercial, scientific and scholarly documents. It even happens in Tolstoy's novel *War and Peace,* when the author starts using French instead of Russian. This too should be detected prior to commencing the translation work, and a decision has to be made as to: (a) Does that text need to be translated? (b) Can the translator handle it? (c) Is it necessary to assign it to another translator?

Once all this preliminary work has been done, one is ready to proceed with the actual translation work.

Depending on the particular text, one should either start translating at this point, or, in the case of a text containing highly specialized terminology which may send the translator on frequent trips to the dictionary, one should first go through the document and make a list of as many unknown or uncertain terms as possible, and then spend some time looking them up and making a word list. This technique saves a great deal of time, since once a list is completed it is much easier to sail through the text, and the time spent initially on making the list is very short compared to the time wasted on repeated interruptions to look up words. Moreover, by first mastering the more difficult terminology of the text, one gains a much better understanding of the subject and is certain to produce a better translation. From the very start, make it a habit to compile word lists and glossaries of subject-specific terminologies, and keep it in a computer database program for future reference. In time, these lists will become your most valuable translation tool.

One should also follow good work habits. Some translators, particularly those engaged in freelance work, tend to overdo it, especially during their "busy season," when they can generate a large income during a relatively short period of time. They will go for twelve or more hours a day, and before they know it they will start complaining of stiffness in the neck and shoulders, blurred vision, and fatigue. One should not translate more than eight hours a day. Six is ideal. Eight is tolerable, provided one takes a few short ten to fifteen minute breaks. Ten is pushing it. Over ten is definitely hazardous to your health.

Before you get ready to submit your translation go over it again, using the following checklist:

Omissions – did you fail to translate any particular word or phrase, or even paragraph?

Format – does your format follow the original (breaking into paragraphs, for instance)?

Mistranslations – did you mistranslate any particular word?

Unknown words – were there words you were not able to translate which you would like to explore further?

Meaning – did you miss the meaning of any phrase or sentence?

Spelling – did you misspell any word which the spell-check function on your computer did not catch?

Grammar – did you make any grammatical mistakes?

Punctuation – did you mispunctuate or miss any punctuation marks?

Clarity – did you fail to clearly convey the meaning of any particular part of the text?

Consistency – did you call something by one name and then by another without any good reason?

"Sound-alike" words – did you mistranslate a word because it looks or sounds like the word in your target language but in reality has a different meaning?

Style – are you satisfied with the way your translation reflects the style of the original text (for example, the original is written in a clear, direct style, while the translation sounds more complex and indirect?)

This checklist is by no means exhaustive, but it does cover the main areas a translator must pay attention to.

As was already explained, your personal computer is your best friend when it comes to translating, editing, and producing a final copy. One can learn a few basic commands, say, in WordPerfect or Microsoft Word, and start using the computer. But there is much more to software than entering, deleting and inserting text. The better acquainted with software you become, the more it will help you with translation. Learn how to do columns and tables, how to use special technical and scientific symbols, do graphic functions, use the spell-check and the thesaurus, create data bases for glossaries and for your own administrative records, and you will tackle a great variety of technical text in many fields at a speed that will amaze you. Remember: speed in translation is the most important thing next to language proficiency. Without it you will not be profitable, and you will be overrun by the competition. With an established record of fast accurate translation you can write your own ticket.

After a few years of using the computer you may want to consider dictation. Personally, I prefer a mix of PC and dictation. When I have an unusually long job and not enough time to do it in, I may revert to dictation. Otherwise, I prefer word-processing. One could argue that by dictating one gets more done and earns more, but there are other things to consider, such as the cost of transcription, the need to edit transcription, and the better control one has over writing than speaking. Some of us are natural speakers; others are writers.

One continues to develop translation techniques over time. One of the most wonderful things about translation, in my opinion, is the fact that your mind is never idle, never in a rut, but rather always being challenged by new tasks, new subjects, new knowledge, and the need to keep up with new developments in language, with different fields of human knowledge, and with the events of the world. As a translator in the Washington area since the late seventies, I have found myself in the middle of world events, beginning with the peace treaty between Egypt and Israel in 1979, when I met Begin, Sadat and Carter, and, more recently, in my daily dealings with events in post-Cold War Eastern Europe, with a strife-torn Middle East, the famine in Somalia, the new North American Free Trade Agreement (NAFTA) between the United States, Canada and Mexico, and the growing involvement of the U.S. space program with the space programs of other nations. Very few people cover as broad an area as a translator. Every day we in the translation business find new challenges, and have to solve new problems. As a result, we are always developing new techniques and finding new answers.

APPENDIX C: TRANSLATOR'S SELF-EVALUATION

The following criteria were developed some years ago by a U.S. Government agency for determin-ing the skill level of a potential translator whom that agency might have liked to hire. You may want to read this chapter carefully to try to make an honest determination as to where on this scale you find yourself at this time. If you are below Level 2+, you need to keep practicing. If you are at Level 3 or higher, you can start doing some professional translating. After Level 4 you are ready for some serious translating, and at Level 5 you can start making a living as a translator.

Translator Skill Levels

Level 0

No functional ability to translate the language. Consistently misunderstanding or cannot comprehend at all.

Level 0+

Can translate all or some place names (i.e., street or city designations), corporate names, numbers and isolated words and phrases,
often translating these inaccurately.

In rendering translations, writes using only memorized material and set expressions. Spelling and representation of symbols (letters, syllables, characters) are frequently incorrect.

Level 1

Sufficient skill to translate the simplest connected written material in a form equivalent to usual printing or typescript. Can translate either representations of familiar formulaic verbal exchanges or simple language containing only the highest-frequency grammatical patterns and vocabulary items, including cognates when appropriate. Translated texts include simple narratives of routine behavior; concrete descriptions of persons, places and things; and explanations of geography and government such as those simplified for tourists. Mistranslations common.

In rendering translations, writes in simple sentences (or clauses), making continual errors in spelling, grammar and punctuation, but translation can be read and understood by a native reader used to dealing with foreigners attempting to translate his/her language.

Level 1+

Sufficient skill to translate simple discourse for informative social purposes in printed form. Can translate material such as announcements or public events, popular advertising notes containing biographical information or narration of events and straightforward newspaper headlines. Has some difficulty with the cohesive factors in discourse, such as matching pronouns with referents.
In rendering translations, writing shows good control of elementary vocabulary and some control of basic syntactic patterns, but major errors still occur when expressing more complex thoughts.

Dictionary usage may still yield incorrect vocabulary of forms, although can use a dictionary to advantage to translate simple ideas. Translations, though faulty, are comprehensible to native readers used to dealing with foreigners.

Level 2

Sufficient skill to translate simple authentic written material in a form equivalent to usual printing. Can translate uncomplicated, but authentic prose on familiar subjects that are normally present in a predictable sequence, which aids the translator in his/her work. Texts may include description and narration in context, such as news items describing frequently occurring events, simple biographical information, social notices, formatted business letters and simple technical material written for the general reader. The prose is predominantly in familiar sentence patterns. Some mistranslations.

In rendering translations, has written vocabulary sufficient to perform simple translations with some circumlocutions. Still makes common errors in spelling and punctuation, but shows some control of the most common formats and punctuation conventions. Good control of morphology of language (in inflected languages) and of the most frequently used syntactic structures. Elementary constructions are usually handled quite accurately, and translations are understandable to a native reader *not* used to reading the translations of foreigners.

Level 2+

Sufficient skill to translate most factual material in nontechnical prose as well as some discussions on concrete topics related to special professional interests. Has begun to make sensible guesses about unfamiliar words by using linguistic context and prior knowledge. May react personally to material, but does not yet detect subjective attitudes, values or judgments in the material to be translated.

In rendering translations, often shows surprising fluency and ease of expression, but under time constraints and pressure language may be inaccurate and/or incomprehensible. Generally strong in either grammar or vocabulary, but not in both. Weaknesses or unevenness in one of the foregoing or in spelling results in occasional mistranslations. Areas of weakness range from simple constructions, such as plurals, articles, prepositions and negatives, to more complex structures, word order and relative clauses. Normally controls general vocabulary, with some misuse of everyday vocabulary still evident. Shows a limited ability to use circumlocutions. Uses dictionary to advantage to supply unknown words. Translations are understandable to native readers not used to dealing with foreigner's attempts to translate the language, though style is obviously foreign.

Level 3

Able to translate authentic prose on unfamiliar subjects. Translating ability is not dependent on subject matter knowledge. Texts will include news stories similar to wire service reports, routine correspondence, general reports and technical material in his/her professional field, all of which include hypothesis, argumentation and supported opinions. Such texts typically include grammatical patterns and vocabulary ordinarily encountered in professional reading.

Mistranslations rare. Almost always able to correctly translate material, relate ideas and make inferences. Rarely has to pause over or reread general vocabulary. However, may experience some difficulty with unusually complex structures and low-frequency idioms.

In preparing translations, control of structure, spelling, and general vocabulary is adequate to convey his/her message accurately, but style may be obviously foreign. Errors virtually never interfere with comprehension and rarely disturb the native reader. Punctuation generally controlled. Employs a full range of structures. Control of grammar good, with only sporadic errors in basic structures, occasional errors in the most complex frequent structures and somewhat more frequent errors in low-frequency complex structures. Consistent control of compound and complex sentences. Relationship of ideas presented in original material is consistently clear.

Level 3+

Increased ability to translate a variety of styles and forms of language pertinent to professional needs. Rarely mistranslates such texts or rarely experiences difficulty relating ideas or making inferences. Ability to comprehend many sociolinguistic and cultural references. However, may miss some nuances and subtleties. Increased ability to translate unusually complex structures and low-frequency idioms; however, accuracy is not complete.

In rendering translations, able to write the language in a few prose styles pertinent to professional/educational needs. Not always able to tailor language to suit original material. Weaknesses may lie in poor control of low-frequency, complex structures, vocabulary or the ability to express subtleties and nuances.

Level 4

Able to translate fluently and accurately all styles and forms of the language pertinent to professional needs. Can translate more difficult prose and follow unpredictable turns of thought readily in any area directed to the general reader and all materials in his/her own special field, including official and professional documents and correspondence. Able to translate precise and extensive vocabulary, including nuances and subtleties, and recognize all professionally relevant vocabulary known to the educated nonprofessional native, although may have some difficulty with slang. Can translate reasonably legible handwriting without difficulty. Understands almost all sociolinguistic and cultural references.

In rendering translations, able to write the language precisely and accurately in a variety of prose styles pertinent to professional/educational needs. Errors of grammar are rare, including those in low-frequency complex structures. Consistently able to tailor language to suit material and able to express subtleties and nuances.

Level 4+

Increased ability to translate extremely difficult or abstract prose. Increased ability to translate a variety of vocabulary, idioms, colloquialisms and slang. Strong sensitivity to sociolinguistic and cultural references. Increased ability to translate less than fully legible handwriting. Accuracy is close to that of an educated translator, but still not equivalent.

In rendering translations, able to write the language precisely and accurately, in a wide variety of prose styles pertinent to professional/educational needs.

Level 5

Can translate extremely difficult and abstract prose (i.e., legal, technical), as well as highly colloquial writings and the literary forms of the language. Translates a wide variety of vocabulary and idioms, colloquialisms, slang and pertinent cultural references. With varying degrees of difficulty, can translate all kinds of handwritten documents. Able to understand how natives think as they produce a text. Accuracy is equivalent to that of a well-educated translator.

In rendering translations, has writing proficiency equal to that of a well-educated native. Without nonnative errors of structure, spelling, style or vocabulary, can translate both formal and informal correspondence, official reports and documents and professional/educational articles, including writing for special purposes which might include legal, technical, educational, literary and colloquial writing.

APPENDIX D: GERMAN TECHNICAL DICTIONARIES

General Dictionaries
Langenscheidts Enzyklopädisches Wörterbuch (Der Große Muret-Sanders) 4 vols., Berlin: Langenscheidt 1990 *The best all-around German-English, English-German dictionary. Quite expensive, but definitely a good investment for the German-English translator.*
Duden Deutsches Universal Wörterbuch, Mannheim: Dudenverlag 1996 *German-German*
Deutsches Wörterbuch, Wahrig, G., Gütersloh: Bertelsmann Lexikon-Verlag 1996 *German-German Excellent reference.*
Brockhaus-Wahrig-Deutsches Wörterbuch, Brockhaus, F.A.,Wiesbaden: 1994
Grosses Abkürzungsbuch, Koblischke, H., Leipzig: VEB Biblio graph-isches Institut Leipzig 1994
Collins German -English English-German Dictionary, Terrell, P., New York: HarperCollins 1993
HarperCollins Unabridged Dictionary (German-English/English-German), New York: HarperCollins 1991
Duden Wörterbuch der Abkürzungen, 2nd rev. ed., von Werlin, J., Mannheim: Dudenverlag 1989 *Recommended.*
Langenscheidts Grosswörterbuch, Messinger H., Berlin: Langenscheidt 1982
The Oxford-Harrap Standard German-English Dictionary, Jones, T., Oxford: Clarendon Press 1977
English-German/German-English Dictionary, 2 vols., Wildhagen Heraucourt, Wiesbaden: Brandstetter Verlag 1972 *Though dated, it is still outstanding.*

German: Acoustics
Dictionary of Acoustics, Langenscheidt, 1992 *English-German/German-English*

German: Advertising/Marketing
Concise Dictionary of Advertising (German-French-English), Koschnick, W.J., 1994
Dictionary of Advertising and Marketing, Gruber, C.M.

German: Aerospace/Aviation
Luftfahrt-Definitionen Englisch-Deutsch/Deutsch-Englisch/Glossary of Aeronautical Terms English-German/German-English 2nd ed., Cescotti, R., Stuttgart: Motorbuch Verlag 1993
Aeronautic & Space Technology Dictionary (Russian-German-English), Kotik, M., 1986

German: Agriculture
Dictionary of Agriculture/Forestry/Horticulture, 2 vols., Langen-scheidt. Vol.1 (English-German) 1990; vol. 2 (German-English) 1993

German: Automotive
Fachwörterbuch der Kfz-Technik, Schmitt, P., Stuttgart/Dresden: Ernst Klett 1992 2 vols. *German-English/English-German Highly recommended.*

German: Biology
German Dictionary of Biology, 2 vols., Eichhorn, Routledge/Langen-scheidt 1998 *Vol. 1 (German-English, 1st ed.); vol. 2 (English-German, 2nd ed.) Scheduled to appear on CD-ROM Spring 1999.*

German: Business and Related Fields
German Dictionary of Business, Commerce and Finance, London: Routledge 1997 *(Also on CD-ROM) German-English/English-German.*

Dictionary of Business & Economics (German-English/English-German), 5th ed., 2 vols. Schäfer, W., Vahlen F. Verlag 1997 (German-English), 1996 (English-German) *Highly recommended; a condensed version is available on CD-ROM.*

Management & Marketing Dictionary (English-German/Geman-English), 2 vols., Schäfer, W., 1995 *Also available on CD-ROM.*

Dictionary of Banking (German-English), Zahn, H.E., 1994

Financial Dictionary (German-English/English-German), Schäfer, W., DTV Verlag 1992

Dictionary of Legal, Commercial and Political Terms, Dietl, Moss & Lorenz, Verlag C.H. Beck 1992 *German-English/English-German. Highly recommended.*

Business German, Clarke, S., New York: HarperCollins 1992

Financial & Economic Glossary (English-German), Zahn, H. 1989

Wörterbuch Wirtschaftsenglisch, Hamblock, D., & Wessels, D.,   German-English 1989; English-German 1990

Cambridge-Eichborn German Dictionary, Cambridge: Eichborn/ Cambridge University Press 1983 *German-English/English-German.*

Wörterbuch der Rechts- und Wirtschaftssprache, Romain, A., Mün-chen: Verlag C.H. Beck 1983 *German-English/English-German*

German: Chemistry

German Dictionary of Chemistry & Chemical Technology, Gross, 2 vols., Routledge/Langenscheidt . Vol. 1 (German-English) 6th ed.: 1997 vol. 2 (English-German) 5th ed. 1997; (*also on CD-ROM 1998*)

German Dictionary of Analytical Chemistry, Knepper et al,   Routledge/Langenscheidt 1997; CD-ROM 1998

Dictionary of Chemistry (German-English/English-German), 2 vols., Wenske, G. German-English 1993; English-German 1992 *The best.*

Chemie und chemische Technik, Technische Universität, Dresden: VEB Verlag Technik 1992 *German-English. Recommended.*

Dictionary of Chemical Engineering, Lydersen, A.L. and Dahl, I. New York: John Wiley and Sons 1992. *English-German-Spanish-French.*

German: Civil Engineering

Dictionary of Building and Civil Engineering, 2 vols., Langenscheidt. Vol. 1 (*English-German, 2nd ed.*): 1995 vol. 2 (*German-English, 1st ed.*)

German: Computers

German Dictionary of Information Technology, London/New York: Routledge 1996; CD-ROM 1997

Computer Englisch Schulze, Herbert, H., Hamburg: Zohwohlt   Taschenbuch Verlag 1997 *German-English/English-German*

Computer Englisch (German-English/English-German), Schulze, H., 1997

Lexikon Informatik und Datenverabeitung/Informatics and Data-processing Lexicon, 4th ed., Schneider, H.J., 1997 *German-English with English-German index.*

Dictionary of Computing (German-English/English-German), Ferretti, V., 1996 *Highly recommended.*

Dictionary of Artificial Intelligence, Langenscheidt 1990 *English-German/German-English*

Technische Kybernetik, Junge, Berlin: VEB Verlag Technik 1982   *English-German/German-English*

Fachausdrücke der Text- und Datenverarbeitung, IBM Deutschland 1978   *English-German*

Fachwörterbuch Energie- und Automatisierungs-Technik, 2 vols., Siemens   *German-English*

Routledge German Dictionary of Information Technology (DC-ROM), Seeburger, U., London: Routledge 1998

German: Construction
German Dictionary of Construction, London/New York: Routledge 1996

German: Electronics
German Dictionary of Electrical Engineering and Electronics, Budig, P.-K., 2 vols., Langenscheidt/Routledge 1998 *Vol. 1 German-English* (6th ed.)*; vol. 2 (5th ed.); (also on CD-ROM)*
German Dictionary of Microelectronics, Bindmann, W., Routledge/ Langenscheidt 1998 *German-English/English-German*

Dictionary of Electronics, Computers & Telecommunications (German-English/English-German), 2 vols., Ferretti, V., 1992
Dictionary of Microelectronics & Microcomputer Technology, Attiyate & Shah, VDI Verlag 1984
Lexikon der Elektronik, Nachrichten und Elektrotechnik, Wernicke, H., Deisenhofen: Verlag H. Wernicke 1979 *German-English-German*

German: Environment
German Dictionary of Environmental Technology, London/New York: Routledge 1997; *(also on CD-ROM)*
Dictionary of Applied Ecology, Langenscheidt 1994
English-German/German-English

German: Food Technology
Dictionary of Food Technology (English-German), Bratfisch, R., Berlin/Paris: Verlag Alexandre Hatier 1992

German: Law
Rechtswörterbuch, 14th ed., Creifelds 1997

Legal Terminology Handbook (Anglo-American-German), Heidinger, F., 1996 *Recommended.*
Legal & Commercial Dictionary, Romain, A., *German-English 1994; English-German 1989*
Dictionary of Legal, Commercial and Political Terms, 2 vols., Dietl, Moss & Lorenz, Verlag C.H. Beck 1992 *German-English/English-German. Recommended.*
Der Grosse Eichborn Legal and Economic Dictionary, Eichborn, R., German-English 1986; English-German 1981

German: Medicine
German Dictionary of Medicine, Nöhring, F-J., 2 vols., Routledge/ Langenscheidt 1997 *Vol.1 (German-English);Vol.2 (English-German); (also on CD-ROM)*
Dictionary of Medicine, Schick, E. New York: ibd Ltd. 1998
Compact Dictionary of Clinical Medicine (English-German), Reuter, P., and C. Reuter 1997
Dictionary of Veterinary Medicine (German-English/English-German), 2nd ed., Mack, R., 1997
Hexal Wörterbuch Medizin German-English/English-German, Walburga, R.B. 1995
English-German Medical Dictionary, Reuter, P. & C. , Stuttgart/New York: Georg Thieme Verlag 1995
Roche Lexikon Medizin, Urban & Schwarzenzberg 1993
Medizinisches Wörterbuch, Unseld, D. *German-English/English-German* 1978
Wörterbuch für Ärtzte, (Dictionary for Physicians) Stuttgart: Georg Thieme Verlag *German-English*

German: Nautical
Schiffstechnisches Wörterbuch, Dluhy, R., Vincentz Verlag 1983 *English-German/German-English*

Schiffahrts Wörterbuch, Hamburg: Horst Kammer   *German-English-French-Spanish-Italian*
German: Nuclear Energy
Engineering, Freyberger, G.H. Stuttgart/New York; Georg Thiemig Verlag 1979   *English-German/German-English.*
Wörterbuch der Kraftwerkstechnik, Konventionelle Dampfkraft-werke, Kernkraftwerke, Stattmann, F., Stuttgart/New York: Georg Thiemig Verlag 1971

German: Optics
Dictionary of Optics and Optical Engineering, 2nd ed., Langenscheidt 1992 *English-German/German-English*

German: Patents
Dictionary of Patent Practice, Üxeküll, J-.D., 1977 *German-English/ English-German*

German: Physics
German Dictionary of Physics, 2 vols., Sube, R., Routledge/ Langen-scheidt . *Vol. 1 (German-English) to appear February 1999; vol. 2 (English-German) to appear February 1999 CD-ROM to appear Fall 1999*

German: Technical
German Technical Dictionary/Universal-Wörterbuch der Technik Englisch, 2 vols., London/New York: Routledge 1997
German-English/English-German; (Also available on CD-ROM and dis-kette)
Fachwörterbuch/Technik und angewandte Wissenschaften German/ English, 5th ed., Walther, R., Berlin/Paris: Verlag Alexandre Hatier 1993
Last Resort Dictionary of Technical Translations (German-English/ English-German), Walker, B., 1992
Dictionary of Engineering and Technology, Ernst, R., Oxford Uni-versity Press 1990. *Recommended.*
Fachwörterbuch Energie und Automatisierungstechnik, Beznei, H., Siemens Aktiengesellschaft 1985
German-English
The Oxford-Duden Pictorial German-English Dictionary, New York: Oxford University Press 1994
The Compact Dictionary of Exact Science and Technology, Kucem, A., Wiesbaden: Brandstetter Verlag 1982   *English-German*
Anglo-American and German Abbreviations in Science and Tech-nology, Wennrich, P., New York: Bowker 1976-78
Solid-State Physics and Electronic Engineering, Bindman, W. 1972 *German-English/English-German*
German-English Technical & Engineering Dictionary, 2nd ed., De Vries, L. & Herrmann, T., New York: McGraw-Hill 1994 *A must for every serious student and translator.*

APPENDIX E: SOURCES OF TRANSLATION WORK

> This book includes a CD (attached to the back cover) with lists of translations companies and international corporations who do a large volume of translation in all languages.

If you choose freelance translation, you should consider yourself a one-person translation company. Your main concern will be where to find work. The need for freelance translation is greater than anyone can estimate, and is clearly growing at a rapid rate. Worldwide, translation is a multibillion dollar industry. But finding translation work on your own is easier said than done. The main problem is that translation is hardly ever a steady, ongoing function of any particular work source, such as an embassy, a company, a government agency, or even a publisher. None of those needs translation every day of the year. Each of them may need a great deal of translation all at once (more than any one person can handle within the given time-frame), and then none for a long time. And, if any one of them needs translation on an ongoing basis, chances are a decision will be made to hire an in-house translator rather than farm out the work.

The fact remains, however, that a well-rounded freelancer can earn well over $50,000 a year, and, in the case of highly specialized technical translators in major languages like Spanish, German, Japanese or Russian, even $100,000 or more. The secret to all of this is establishing for yourself a good clientele. There are two ways of doing this. The first, and by far the hardest, is finding your own clients and working with them directly. You may want to contact embassies, law firms, publishers, government agencies and so on, and solicit work directly from them. If you are fortunate enough to find some good steady clients on your own, you will be doing quite well. But the problem often lies in the word "steady." What seems to be a steady client today may not be so steady tomorrow.

This brings us to the second, and by far the safer option, which is translation agencies. There are hundreds of them in the United States, and they handle huge amounts of translation business every year. In this chapter we will discuss translation agencies, as well as direct sources of translation available to the freelancer.

Translation Agencies

Translation agencies, also known as translation companies, or translation bureaus, are for the most part privately owned commercial establishments ranging in size from one or two employees to ten or more, but hardly ever larger than ten. Some are divisions of larger companies, such as Berlitz, which is primarily a language school and publisher, offering translation as a secondary function. Some specialize in one language only, such as Spanish, German, or Japanese. Most offer several languages, and quite a few bill themselves as offering "all languages." This last type is somewhat pretentious, since there are more languages in the world than any one person can identify. But what they really mean is that they will make the effort to find a translator in almost any language they may be called upon to translate.

As a general rule, translation agencies employ relatively few in-house translators, since the flow of work in any given language is usually uneven. Instead, they rely on the services of a network of hundreds of freelancers who can handle a great variety of subjects. Those freelancers are located all over the United States and even abroad. The ones who are most reliable and professional get the major share of the work, and some of them earn the above-quoted figures.

As a freelancer, you need to cultivate at least one such agency, preferably two or three. The problem in working with only one is that, with few exceptions, there may not be a steady flow of work coming out of any given agency in any given language, in subjects you are equipped to handle. Two or three will give you better coverage, and assure a better flow. On the other hand, you may find yourself in a situation where all three ask you to do something at the same time, and you may not be able to do it. You need to establish an understanding with your agencies that would make an allowance for such a scenario, so that you don't spoil your relationship with any one of them.

The worst thing you can do as a freelancer working with translation agencies is to overcommit yourself. Your most important personal asset is your reliability. Once you fail to meet deadlines (keep in mind—the agency stands to lose a client if deadlines are not met), your reliability becomes questionable, and if you do it once too often, you may soon find out that those phone calls from the agency offering you work assignments stop coming.

Where do you look for translation agencies? Starting on page 112 you will find a listing of hundreds of such agencies. You can find more in the Yellow Pages, or through the ATA (American Translators Association), which has local chapters around the country. My suggestion is to start with those close to home. In this day and age of international electronic communications, distance has little meaning. But then again, close to home still works, because you can meet the people there, befriend them, and in some instances even avail yourself of their dictionaries and other resources.

Keep in mind that a translation company has overhead, and also needs to make some profit to stay in business. They do the hard work of finding translation assignments, and therefore share with you the profit from the job. You can usually make more money by going directly to the client, and if you have enough of your own clients you don't need a translation company to send work your way. But most freelance translators do need those companies, which invariably provide a more steady flow of work than what a freelancer can get on his or her own.

The two things all translation companies appreciate and reward in a freelancer are honesty and loyalty. If you agree to a deadline, stick to it. Don't renege on it at the last minute. That's a sure prescription to spoil your association with your company. Equally important is not to go behind the company's back and try to solicit its own clients directly. Some companies will make you sign an agreement to this effect. Others will rely on the honor system. Don't abuse their trust. It usually doesn't pay off.

Direct Sources of Work

Working with translation agencies usually does not stop you from finding your own clients, as long as there is no conflict of interest with the agency's clients. It would be impossible to list here all the potential sources of direct translation work, since they include practically the entire human race (everyone needs a document translated at some point). But there are some major sources which ought to be mentioned, and here are some of the more important ones.

Schreiber Translations, Inc.

PO Box 4193 • Rockville, Maryland 20849 • Phone: 301.424.7737 • Fax: 301.424.2336
visit our website at www.schreiberNet.com

Dear Prospective Translator:

Thank you for your interest in working with Schreiber Translations, Inc. Upon receipt of your resume, we are interested in finding our more specific information regarding your services. This information will enable us to better match our needs with your services.

Our company specializes in highly technical translation in over 50 languages. Most of the time, we work under strict time constraints, and our deadlines are critical. To qualify as a freelance translator, you need expertise in specific areas, native ability in your target-language, current electronic equipment, and a commitment to deadlines and quality.

To help you evaluate the above requirements, please fill out the following questionnaire and fax or mail it back as soon as possible.

Your Name: _____ **S.S.#** _____

Address: _____

City: _____ **State:** _____ **Zip:** _____

Phone: _____ **Work:** _____ **FAX:** _____ **E-Mail:** _____

QUESTIONNAIRE:

Language(s) you translate into English:

_____

Language(s) you translate from English:

_____

Subjects you specialize in (circle each subject):

Aerospace	Maritime	Military	Civil Engineering
Medical	Legal	Computers	Telecommunications
Chemistry	Mathematics	Physics	Business/Finance
Political	Energy	Environmental	Patents (medical, chemical mechanical)
Social Sciences	Agriculture		

Other (please specify):_____

What rates do you charge for each language combination:

_____

Language(s) you interpret into/from English:

_____

Type of interpretation you have experience in (circle each area):

Consecutive	Simultaneous	Conference	Escort

OVER ➔

Questionnaire sent by a translation agency to translators inquiring about freelance work

---

What rates do you charge for each type of interpretation?

_____

Your last main translation/interpretation assignments during the past 12 months (please indicate subject, size, and approximate time it took to accomplish):

1. _____

2. _____

3. _____

Equipment: (please check appropriate boxes):

☐ IBM or IBM-compatible   ☐ Microsoft Word 6.0
☐ WordPerfect 5.1   ☐ Microsoft Word 7.0
☐ WordPerfect 6.0/6.1   ☐ Power Point Version
☐ WordPerfect 8.0   ☐ Desktop Publishing
☐ Modem   ☐ Typesetting
☐ Fax   ☐ Internet Capabilities
☐ Laser Printer
☐ Foreign language software (please specify): _____

Other Programs: _____

How many words or pages per day can you translate in your language(s) of expertise, please spec

_____

_____

What else can you tell us about yourself that would enhance your posture as an experienced freel translator:

_____

_____

_____

Would you be willing to do a short test paragraph in any of the language(s) and subject(s) you hav listed above? (please specify):

_____

_____

Do you work on a full-time basis somewhere other than your home? If so, can you receive calls th At what number?

_____

Thank you for taking the time to answer fill out this questionnaire. We hope to have the opportul working with you in the future.

Reverse side of the questionnaire

SCHREIBER TRANSLATIONS, INC.
51 Monroe Street, Suite 101
Rockville, MD 20850
Phone: (301) 424-7737

WORK ORDER
Fax: (301) 424-2336
Modem: (301) 424-0877
E-Mail: Translation@schreiberNet.com

JOB NO. STI-24000   Date Assigned: 08/02/99   Date Due: **09/01/99**
12:00:00 PM

NAME   JOHN DOE
ADDRESS   1234 MAIN STREET
              WASHINGTON, DC   USA

PHONE H: 202.555.1234   **FAX:** 202.555.1234

SERVICES REQUIRED:
☒ Translation   ☐ Editing   ☐ Proofreading   ☐ Formatting   ☐ Dictation
LANGUAGE (FROM) **SPANISH**   (TO) **ENGLISH**
NOTE: IMMEDIATELY CHECK MATERIAL RECEIVED FROM STI FOR ANY OMISSIONS.

REQUESTED   ☐ Hard Copy   ☒ **Electronic Copy with file name 24000-SP.DOC**
DELIVERABLE:
DELIVERY: ☒ E-Mail   ☐ Facsimile   ☐ Modem   ☐ Overnight

SPECIAL INSTRUCTIONS:

NOTE: THIS DOCUMENT IS FOR BILLING PURPOSES ONLY. NOTES OR COMMENTS OF ANY KIND RELATING TO THIS JOB SHOULD BE
RELAYED DIRECTLY TO THE PROJECT MANAGER. INCLUDING THEM HERE MAY DELAY PAYMENT.

GENERAL INSTRUCTIONS: (PLEASE READ CAREFULLY):
- The due date specified above is binding. If unable to meet deadline, inform STI immediately by phone so that appropriate action may be taken. Extensions will be granted whenever possible. Late delivery may result in adjustment of payment.
- All work is considered confidential and should not be discussed without STI authorization
- Translator is responsible for providing a complete and accurate translation, free of spelling errors, omissions, and grammatically and idiomatically poor language. Translator is responsible for reproducing all numbers unless otherwise agreed. STI reserves the right to reject unacceptable work and/or request improvements prior to payment. An incomplete or inaccurate translation may result in adjustment of payment or, in extreme cases non-payment.
- Contractor is required to keep a backup file and/or hard copy of all jobs for up to one month following delivery.
Payment: Payroll is issued on the 15th of every month. All work submitted on or before the 15th of a given month will be paid on the 15th of the following month. Any work submitted to STI after the 15th will be paid on the second 15th thereafter. Payment for written translations is based on target language word count according to agreed program(s), unless otherwise agreed and specified. Payment for editing, proof-reading or formatting will be agreed upon before acceptance of job.

**THIS PORTION OF THE FORM MUST BE FILLED IN, THE BOTTOM MUST BE SIGNED, AND THE FORM MUST BE RETURNED TO STI
FOR PAYMENT TO BE EFFECTED.**

PLEASE CHECK THE FOLLOWING:
☐ DID YOU EDIT YOUR WORK?   ☐ DID YOU DOUBLE CHECK NUMBERS?
☐ DID YOU SPELL CHECK YOUR WORK?   ☐ DID YOU CHECK FOR OMMISIONS?
☐ DID YOU USE SPECIFIED FORMAT?   ☐ DID YOU NAME YOUR FILE 24000-SP.DOC?

TOTAL: WORDS/HOURS/PAGES   X $ (RATE) = $

THANK YOU FOR YOUR CONTINUED SUPPORT.

SIGNATURE OF CONTRACTOR   DATE SUBMITTED   APPROVED BY

THIS FORM MUST BE SIGNED AND RETURNED TO SCHREIBER TRANSLATIONS, INC. IN ORDER FOR PAYMENT TO BE EFFECTIVE

Translation agency's work order

Law Firms

Law firms are a major source of translation work. Some of the larger firms hire full-time translators or staff members who are bilingual, especially if they do business on a regular basis with a foreign entity. Most firms use translators on an as-needed basis. Legal translation is a specialized field in which you need to acquire experience working with legal documents. There are several legal specialties, such as patent law, international law, immigration, and so on. Each specialty has its own style and terminology, which a translator needs to become acquainted with. As a freelancer, adding legal translation to your list of specialties is an excellent idea. You will find out that your volume of translation will increase considerably by doing so.

Quite often, a law firm needs both document translation and interpretation. Keep in mind that interpretation is a discipline separate from translation, and that there is a big difference between one-on-one consecutive interpreting and simultaneous conference interpreting. If asked by a law firm to do both text translation and interpreting, be sure to find out first exactly what the assignments consist of.

Industry

Corporations doing business in other countries have to deal with documents originated in the languages of those countries or English documents that need to be translated into those languages. Here again we find the two approaches of either hiring translators or farming out work to freelancers and to translation services (or a combination of both). This field is perhaps the fastest growing source of translation in the closing years of the twentieth century. More and more major American companies are turning to international business as a way to offset the decline of business at home and to gain a share of the world market. Their need for translation is growing every day, and even those who have in-house translators are finding themselves using freelancers because of their volume of translation work.

If you are fortunate enough to form a relationship with a major company doing business overseas, you may find yourself in the enviable position of dealing with a major, steady source of translation.

How does one get work with major corporations? If you have a special expertise in their field of work, say you are a telecommunications expert and you would like to translate for Sprint, find out who handles outside vendors or services, and give them a call or drop them a note. It also helps to know someone in the company, who can do some of the legwork for you and put you in touch with the right people. As a general rule, this is not easy to do. But persistence does pay off some of the time, and even if only a few respond, it is worth the effort.

The U.S. Government

For several decades following World War Two, translation in the federal government enjoyed a boom. The onset of the Cold War resulted in wide-scale translation activities on the part of the U.S. Department of Defense (DoD), all the branches of the service (particularly the Army, Navy, and Air Force), and the Central Intelligence Agency (CIA). In addition, such multilingual organizations as the Voice of America (which started broadcasting in 1942 in 40 languages), sprang into being. These and other organizations employed a host of translators, and farmed out millions of words every year to be translated. Looking back, those were the feast years of government translation. During the nineties, however, a major shift has been taking place. Since 1992, there has been a sharp decline in government translations, and those translation agencies and freelancers who were dependent on government work for their bread and butter, are hurting. This is not to say that the U.S. Government is no longer a source of employment for translators. There are still many opportunities for translation in the government, offered by such bodies as the Language Services division of the U.S. Department of State (for in-house as well as freelance translators and interpreters), the Library of Congress, the U.S. Patent and Trademark Office, and so on (see list of U.S. Government Agencies, Appendix 4).

My translation company, Schreiber Translations, Inc. (STI), started out in life as a full-service translation company for the federal government. This was in the early eighties, when the boom was still on. We provided translation from and into over 50 languages and dialects, as well as interpreting, transcription, voice-over, graphics, and editing. Luckily for us, we realized early on that, as the world was changing, we were better off not being locked into government work, and we were able to develop a lucrative practice in the nongovernmental sectors. Today, government work makes up less than 50% of our total translation work.

What does all of this mean to linguists seeking translation work in the closing years of the twentieth century? There is no one simple answer. The government has been known to swing like a fast-moving pendulum. This author believes that before long the federal government will be launching new major translation projects, in such sectors as world trade and international relations. American interaction with other cultures and languages is far from diminishing. If anything, it is increasing day by day. One good example is the American space program, conducted by the National Aeronautics and Space Administration (NASA). Back in the sixties, there were two major space programs in the world—the Soviet and the American. Today, many countries in Western Europe and Asia have an active space program, and many of them are involved in cooperative efforts. NASA is actively involved in this new international space scene, and the need for translation in this particular organization should not be underestimated. But all of this, of course, is speculative. The federal government is making a historical effort to reduce its enormous deficit, and since the lawmakers of our land are not necessarily attuned to the critical importance of translation, translation may well be a casualty of the budget wars. Translators would be well advised not to write off doing translation for the government, since it is, and will continue to be, the single biggest employer around. But they should put at least as much, if not more, effort into finding translation work outside the government, where indeed the field is all but limitless.

What are the pros and cons of translating for the government? For many linguists over the years, the government has offered job security. I know some fine translators who have worked for the government for many years and had interesting and fulfilling careers. On the other hand, career translators in the government are not paid exceptionally high salaries. Quite a few freelance on the side in an effort to supplement their income. As for freelancers who contract with the government, here we have mixed results. Some have found themselves a cozy niche and are kept busy on a fairly regular basis. Others go through the "feast and famine" syndrome. Some have been frustrated by spending a long time hunting for government assignments, with little result. To freelance effectively for the government, one should, in most instances, work in one of the top five languages the U.S. Government is interested in (Spanish, Russian, German, French and Japanese). Any other language, even Chinese or Arabic, may not offer enough of a flow. One should also make many contacts.

On the downside, government agencies, with few exceptions, are notorious for not paying on time. A few years ago, the government passed a "prompt payment" act, which mandates 30-day net payment, with interest accruing thereafter. The problem is, more than a few agencies take at least another 30 days to process an invoice, claiming that it takes that long to get your invoice "into the system." Others take even longer, and simply neglect to add interest. If you try to get it, you may soon find out you waste more time going after it than it's worth. In some extreme cases—which are by no means rare—it can take six to twelve months to get paid. Your invoice simply gets lost in the system. Your remedy is to contact your congressperson, who will call that particular government office to make sure you get paid. The problem is, those folks in the finance office often resent being put on the spot in this manner, and while they will expedite your payment, you may not get work next time. It all sounds shocking, but having been there, it is my civic duty to let you know.

Another drawback of government freelancing is the incredible amount of paperwork you are asked to fill out in doing some of those jobs. I have done five and ten dollar jobs that required three detailed forms filled out, plus an invoice in six copies, mailed to three different offices (finance, procurement, and contract). It took me longer to do the paperwork than to translate, and clearly the whole thing was not worth my while. If you do a fair amount of freelancing for the government, you learn to overlook these excesses. Otherwise, you may have to decide whether it's all worth it.

A third major drawback to doing government work is the fact that quite often the translation standards of a particular agency may be quite low. As a result, you run the risk of developing poor translation habits, lack of attention to details, lack of sufficient editing and proofing, and so on. What that means in a practical sense is that when a more demanding job comes along, especially in the private sector, you may find out your performance is not satisfactory, and you may lose your client.

Having said all this, it behooves me to add that during the last seventeen years I have interacted with hundreds of government employees and dozens of agencies, and many of those have been a delight to work with, and overall I have been very fortunate to have this unique opportunity to take part in many historical events, including the peace treaty between Israel and Egypt, the Gulf War, the disarmament agreement with the former Soviet Union, the Bosnian peace agreement, and many more. Thus, working with the government as a linguist is by no means a dull experience, and if you learn how to take some of the problems in your stride, you can do quite well.

State and Local Government

Government at all levels, from the municipal to the federal, needs translation. At the local level we find more and more city and county government translating their pamphlets, brochures and other documents into the languages of their immigrant populations, notably Asian languages and Spanish. In addition, local government has an ongoing need for interpreters, mostly for the court system, but also for social services, hospitals, and other local institutions. At this time of tight budgets, this may not be the most lucrative field, but it is definitely worth exploring, since it is local, and mostly uses local linguists.

Major Organizations

Among the largest organizations that use a great deal of translation one should mention the United Nations, The World Bank, the World Health Organization, the Organization of American States, to cite only some of the better-known ones here in the U.S. Surely there are more in Europe, such as the World Court, the European Community, NATO, and many more. Most of these organizations use in-house linguists, and do not farm out translation work if they can help it. But quite often they have more documents to translate than they can handle in-house, and they look for outside help.

For a list of such organizations and how to contact them, see Appendix 4.

Publishers

Book publishers use freelance translators in many different ways. This is not an easy field to break into, particularly for the beginner. Many publishers turn to academia for translators, and if you are in academia and can translate from or into another language in your field of expertise, there is a chance you can get the work. Others turn to established translators with name recognition. But it is certainly worth trying, to query publishers and find out if they need your services.

Software Localization Companies

A fast-growing area of translation is software localization, or translation of software-related text into other languages and adapting the text to the target culture. Software localization companies specialize in computer subjects and in English-into-foreign language translation. They employ in-house translators, but they also use freelancers from time to time. Their work encompasses everything from computer manuals to localization of web-sites.

Networking

An excellent source of work for freelance translators is personal contacts with other translators. The ATA's local chapters are one place where translators meet and get to know each other. The annual conference of the ATA holds a networking session, which is very valuable. One also meets

translators through personal contacts in the translation field.

The latest way to meet translators is on the Internet. Entities such as the Foreign Language Forum on CompuServe bring together translators from all over the world. All you need to do is post a message on one of those programs, and before you know it you get a response from someone in your own town or half way around the world.

Keeping in touch with other translators is a prime means of finding out about work sources and assignments. There are clearly many advantages to networking in the translation field, and the more contacts one has the better.

The following is a listing of translation companies in the United States and Canada which use freelance translators. None of the companies is rated. It is up to you to find out which company best meets your needs.

-A-

A E Inc. Translations, 14780 Memorial Drive, Ste. 202, Houston, TX 77079-5284 Phone: (281)870-0677 Fax: (281)556-9737 e-mail: aeinc @phoenix.net Web site: aetrans.com Contact: Stephen D. Ross, President Member: ATA

AA Translation Express, 1018 Gott St., Ann Arbor, MI 48103 Phone: (734)665-7295 Fax: (734)665-1345 e-mail: univtrans@mediaone. net Contact: Laurie Finch

AAA Translators, Inc., 3030 Elmore Park Rd., Memphis, TN 38134-3606 Phone: (901)372-7373 Fax: (901)372-7020 e-mail: aaa@translators. com Gabriel O'Meara, President Contact: Bobby Lahiere, Project Manager
Founded 1991, company is moving into its own headquarters in 1999. Its main languages (both ways) are Spanish, Portuguese, French, and Italian. Additional languages are German and Arabic. Main items translated are technical manuals, MSDS'. Specialized aeas include engineering, employee handbooks, chemical, videos, voice overs. Annual workload is about 2.5 million words a year. Utilizes about 1000 translators. Prospective translators should submit a resume. Resumes are filed by category, language, and experience.

Academy Translations, 156 River Rd., Studio 6, Mansfield Center, CT 06250-1015 Phone: (860)429-2070 Fax: (860)429-8521 email: acadtran @snet.net Contact: David J. Marsh, Director of Operations
Founded 1996. Member: ATA, NAJIT. Translates all languages, both from and into English. Emphasis on all areas of translation, with specialties in Business and Finance, Insurance and Banking, Manufacturing, Immigration and Naturalization and Broadcast and Print Journalism. Prospective translators should demonstrate proficiency in their languages, and be able to verify their education and experience. ATA or other accreditation is preferred. Resumes are evaluated, and if qualified, translators are sent a letter with a subcontractual agreement. **Academy Translations** maintains a pool of 650 translators. The company's services also include proofreading/editing, desktop publishing, narration and dubbing. Translation accounts for about 50% of the work, and interpreting has been increasing. With 1500 translators and interpreters in their pool, they are looking to add more.

Access Language Experts, 865 United Nations Plaza, New York, NY 10017 Phone:(212)818-1102 Fax:(212)818-1265 e-mail: alxusa@aol.com Contact: Ken Clark
Founded 1990. Translates all languages. Translators must be experienced professionals. Receipt of resumes followed up by phone or mail. Resumes must be e-mailed to: resume@languageexperts.com

Accuworld LLC, 433 South Main St., Ste. 308, West Hartford, CT 06107 Tel. (860)561-3388 Fax (860)561-7247 e-mail: sjoyce@ inlinguahtfd.com Contact: Susan Joyce, Excecutive Director
Founded 1988. Affiliated with Inlingua. Uses freelance translator and interpreters. Accepts unsolicited resumes. Resumes kept on file. Applicants receive information packets. Translators are expected to be native speakers. Main languages are Portuguese and Vietnamese. Additional languages are Spanish, German, Polish, Russian, Chinese, Italian, and French. Main subjects are legal, technical, and scientific. Provides cross-cultural services in addition to translation/interpretation.

ACE Translation Center, 200 Roy St., #100, Seattle, WA 98109
Phone: (206)216-0786 Fax: (206) e-mail: atc@cultural.org Web site: cultural.org Contact: Maya Vengadasalam Member: ATA

Action Translation Bureau, 7825 West 101ˢᵗ St., Palos Hills, IL 60465 Phone: (708)598-9124
All languages, all subjects.

AD-EX WORLDWIDE, 525 Middlefield Rd., Ste. 150, Menlo Park, CA 94025-3458 Phone: (650)854-6732 Fax: (650)325-7409 e-mail: 76620.3521@compuserve.com Web site: industrynet/ad-ex. worldwide
Founded 1957. Member: ATA. Translates in all major languages, in all industrial fields, especially in the power and aerospace industries. Prospective translators must have demonstrable years of experience and written evidence of competence, including resumes and work samples. Resumes are responded to with a request for samples which are then thoroughly examined. **AD-EX** maintains a pool of "hundreds" of translators. The company is always glad to hear from veteran professional translators. Their client base is worldwide.

Adams Technical Translations, 10435 Burnet Rd., Ste. 125, Austin, TX 78758 Phone:(512)821-1818 Fax:(512)821-1888 e-mail: mail @adamstrans.com Web site: adamstrans.com Contact: Leigh Yeager, Project Manager
Founded 1982. Member: ATA, AATIA, AITA. Translates English into French, Spanish, German, Chinese, Japanese, Italian, Portuguese, Korean, Russian, and Dutch. Emphasis on Hardware, Software, Legal, Engineering, Medical and Patent translations. Prospective translators should be native speakers with college/ graduate degree in that language and training or experience in specialized technical area(s). Resumes are entered in a database and called as possible jobs come up. **Adams** maintains a pool of 1000+ translators. The company also has desktop publishing and hypertext services.

Agnew Tech-II, 741 Lakefield Rd., Ste. C, Westlake Village, CA 91361-2618 Phone: (805)494-3999 Fax: (805)494-6849 e-mail: agnewi @agnew.com Web site: agnew.com Contact: Irene Agnew
Founded 1986. Member: ATA, NAWBO. Translates Spanish, Chinese, French, German, Japanese, Russian, Vietnamese, etc. from English. Covers all technical areas. Prospective translators should have a B.A. degree or higher and 2-3 years experience. Resumes are reviewed, graded and scheduled for a translation test. **Agnew** maintains a pool of 300 translators. The company is a full-service translation bureau, as well as providing desktop publishing, web page design, multimedia, and audiovisual services.

Albors and Associates, Inc., P.O. Box 5516 Winter Park, FL 32793 Phone: (800)785-8634 / (407)678-8634 Fax: (407)657-7004 e-mail: rene@albors.com René Albors, President Contact: Carlos Bertizlian, Vice President
Founded 1996. Member: ATA, NAJIT, Hispanic Chamber of Commerce, Orlando Chamber of Commerce. Translates Spanish, French, Portuguese, Japanese, German, Chinese, Russian, Polish, Arabic and Italian, both from and into English. Emphasis on Legal, Medical and Business translations. Prospective translators should be experienced, expert with terminology, and prompt in their delivery of finished work. Accepts unsolicited resumes for translation and interpretation. Resumes are computer-filed, and a letter of thanks is sent to acknowledge receipt. **Albors & Associates** maintains a pool of 1300 translators.

All-Language Services, 545 Fifth Ave., New York, NY 10017 e-mail: alsny@idt.com Web site: all-language.com   Phone: (212)986-1688 Fax: (212)986-3396 Patricia Besner, President Contact: Miriam Edgelow, Personnel
Founded 1959. Uses freelance translators and interpreters. Accepts unsolicited resumes. If interested, asks for work sample, and offers a small initial assignment. Applicant must be a professional translator. Main languages (both ways) are Spanish, French, Italian, German, Portuguese, Chinese, Korean, Japanese, Dutch, and Russian. In total, some 59 languages. Main subjects are finance, law, advertising, banking, including brochures, annual reports, and manuals. Uses 80 translators in house, and some 1000 on call.

ALTA Language Services, 3355 Lennox Rd. NE, Ste. 510, Atlanta, GA 30326 Phone: (888)302-4455 Fax: (800)895-7633 Abe Revitch, Owner Contact: Robert Jones

Company founded 1982. Member: ATA, AAIT. Uses freelance translators and interpreters. Accepts unsolicited resumes. Resumes are filed by language. Requires outstanding translation skills. Main languages (both ways) are Spanish, German, French, Japanese, Portuguese, Dutch, Italian, Chinese, Korean, and Russian. Main subjects are legal, medical, and general. Engages around 300 translators. Does multilingual typesetting in addition to translation and interpretation.

ALTCO Translations, 1426 Ridgeview Rd., Columbus, OH 43221 Phone: (614)486-2014 Fax: (614)486-6940 e-mail: trudypeters@ compuserve.com Contact: Trudy E. Peters, Owner.
Founded 1982. Member: ATA. Uses freelancers for translation and interpretation. Accepts resumes, and enters the more promising ones into a database. Applicants must be experienced. Main languages (both ways) are Spanish, French, German, Russian, and Japanese. Also translates into other languages, notably Italian. Main subjects are patents, business documents, manuals, certificates, brochures. Uses dozens of translators.

Amway Corporation, 7575 East Fulton Rd., Ada, MI 49355 Phone:(616)787-6113 Fax:(616)787-4446 Modem: (616)682-4033 Contact: Reinhard Epp, Translation Department
Company founded 1959. Member: ATA. Translates Spanish, French, German, Italian, Dutch, Japanese, Chinese, Korean, Portuguese, Hindi, Polish, Hungarian, Czech, Slovak, Slovene, Turkish, Indonesian, Vietnamese, Malay, and Russian both from and into English. Bulk of work in Spanish and French. Emphasis on Marketing literature, Legal documentation, Product-related materials (Labels, brochures), Technical documentation (chemical and biological topics). Prospective translators should have at least 3-5 years full-time experience as a translator and/or interpreter. ATA accreditation preferred. Resumes are placed in a database. **Amway** maintains a pool of 200-300 translators.

APS International Ltd, 7800 Glenroy Rd., Minneapolis, MN 55439-3122 Phone: (612)831-7776 Contact: Translation Department

ASIST Translation Services, 4663 Executive Drive, Ste. 11, Columbus, OH 43220 Phone: (614)451-6744 Fax: (614)451-1349 e-mail: asist@asisttranslations.com Web site: assisttranslations.com Contact: Elena Tsinman, President
Company founded 1983. Member: ATA. Uses freelance translators and interpreters. Accepts unsolicited resumes. All resumes are entered in a database. If qualified, translator is contacted immediately. Applicant must be experienced, native speaker, and have a university degree. Main languages are English into Spanish, French, Italian, Portuguese, Chinese, Japanese, Arabic, Korean, Dutch, Finnish, German. Additional languages are Russian, Swedish, Hungarian, Czech, Slovak, and more. Does 5-7 million words a year. Maintains pool of 400-500 translators. Does also typesetting, Web site translation, software translation, localization, audio-visual productions, and desktop publishing.

Atlas Translation Services, 336 North Central Ave., Ste. 6, Glendale, CA 91203 Phone: (818)242-2400 Fax: (818)242-2475 e-mail: atlas @atlaspus.com Ted Ziafathy, owner Contact: Sorina Kalili
Founded 1993. Uses freelancers for translation. Accepts unsolicited resumes. Main languages (both ways) are Farsi, German, Spanish, French, Arabic, Chinese, and Japanese. Main subjects are legal, business, and scripts. Also does legal interpretation.

-B-

Barinas Translation Consultants, Inc., PO Box 163424, San Antonio, TX 78280-2624] Phone: (210)545-0019 Fax: (210)545-4731 160424 E-mail: info@barinas.com Web site: barinas.com Contact: Sonia Barinas, President
Company founded 1980. Member: MPI, AAHA, TSHE, SATC, San Antonio Chamber of Commerce, GSHMA, ISMP, THMA. Uses freelance translators and interpreters. Accepts unsolicited resumes. Resumes are checked for quality and experience, then filed by language and areas of expertise. Please submit sample with resume, and indicate degree in translation and/or interpretation. Degree in law, medicine etc. is a plus. Main language pairs are Spanish/English, French/ English, French/Spanish, Portuguese/English, German/English, Chinese/English, Japanese/English. Main subjects are legal, medical, technical, telecom. Specializes in simultaneous interpretation for

meetings and conventions. Does about 350 projects a year. Uses hundreds of freelancers.

BBC Multilingual Translations, 1231 Somerset Drive, McLean, VA 22101-2336 Phone: (703)448-0893 Fax: (703)448-8077 e-mail: mansourf @aol.com

Berkeley Scientific Translation Service, Inc., 2748 Adeline St., Ste. D, Berkeley CA 94704 Phone:(510)548-4665 Fax: (510)548-4666 e-mail: marlo@berksci.com Web site: berksci.com Contact: Kai Simonsen, Translation Coordinator
Founded 1974. Member: ATA, NCTA. Translates Japanese, Korean, Chinese, and other major European and Asian languages, both from and into English. Emphasis on Mechanical, Automotive, Chemical and Chemical Engineering, Computers and Software, Electronics, Biotechnology, Pharmaceuticals, Physics and Patent translations. Prospective translators should be able to produce authoritative translations into their native language within a specialized area. Resumes are screened for educational background and subject expertise as related to translation experience. Berkeley maintains a pool of 70-100 translators. The company was founded by a physicist and engineer and seeks translators with similar qualifications.

Berlitz operates at the following addresses:
    525 Broadway Ste. 300, Santa Monica, CA 90401-2419
    1730 Rhode Island Ave. NW, Washington, DC 20036
    396 Alhambra Circle, Coral Gables, FL 33134
    2 North LaSalle St., Chicago, IL 60602
    61 Broadway, New York, NY 10006
    257 Park Ave. S., New York, NY 10010
    580 Walnut St., Cincinnati, OH 45202
    1608 Walnut St., Philadelphia, PA 19103
    8400 North Mo-Pac Expressway, Austin, TX 78759
    520 Post Oak Blvd., Houston, TX 77027
    5815 Callaghan Rd., San Antonio, TX 78229
    2070 Chain Bridge Rd., Tysons Corner, VA 22103
Berlitz is an international organization of language schools which offer translation services as a sideline. Most of its branches use the services of freelance translators. Berlitz is very active in the localization of software. Prospective translators should definitely consider contacting this company. Check out its Web site at: berlitz.com.

BioMedical Translators, 3477 Kenneth Drive, Palo Alto, CA 94303 Phone:(650)494-1317 Fax:(650)494-1394 e-mail: biomed@biomedical.com Contact: Recruitment Department
Founded 1992. Member: ATA, NCTA. Main languages translated are French, German, Italian, Spanish, Dutch, Swedish, Portuguese, Danish, Japanese, and Chinese. Emphasis is on Medical and Biological translation, including equipment, studies and software. Prospective translators should possess at least one year experience, have knowledge of the medical field, and have access to medical dictionaries. Their equipment should include a PC and modem or e-mail; software should include Word and WordPerfect. Resumes are reviewed by the recruiting department and responded to with a test translation, which is then evaluated. **BioMedical** maintains a pool of 500+ translators. The company specializes exclusively in the medical field and its peripherals. Their services also include desktop publishing.

Bowne Translation Services, 345 Hudson St., New York, NY 10014 Phone: (212)924-5500 Fax: (212)229-3410 e-mail: harry.qiu@bowne.com Web site: bowne.com Lisa Di Meglio, Managing Director Contact: Harry Qiu, Director of Operations
Company founded 1989. Member: ATA. Uses freelance translators and interpreters. Accepts unsolicited resumes. Applicants sign a confidentiality agreement and are sent a test. If successful, they are given small assignments at first, leading to larger ones. Main language pairs are English into Spanish, Ger-man, French, Chinese, Japanese, and Portuguese, and Spanish, French, German, and Japanese into English. Additional languages are Italian, Dutch, Swedish, Danish, Norwegian, Greek, Polish, Hungarian, Czech, Bulgarian, and Tagalog. Main subjects are financial, legal, corporate, and industrial, as well as documents related to IPO/mergers and acquistions. Keeps about 400-500 translators in its pool.

-C-

Comprehensive Language Center (formerly **CACI Language Center**), 4200 Wilson Blvd., Ste. 950, Arlington VA 22203 Phone: (703)247-0700 Fax: (703)247-4295 e-mail: mswymelar@hg.caci.com Web site: comlang.com Robert W. Neil, President Contact: Marta Swymelar, Vice President
Company founded 1980 as CACI. Member: ATA. uses freelance translators and interpreters. Accepted unsolicited resumes, but not unsolicited phone calls. Qualified applicants are sent a database form which is processed and are called upon when needed in their area of expertise. Requirements include college degree, 2 years professional experience as linguist, or appropriate certification/specialized degree. Over 100 languages. Main areas are technical, legal, promotional, business. Company also does training, transcription, software and web page localization, and video narration.

Calderon Language Translators, 4133 South Wheeling Ave., Tulsa, OK 74105 Phone:(918)743-3692 Fax: (918)743-3667 Contact: Brenda
Founded 1973. Translates Spanish, French, German, Russian, Chinese, Russian, Vietnamese, Italian, Japanese, Portuguese, Polish, Dutch, Swedish, and Norwegian both from and into English. Also Arabic into English. Emphasis on Engineering, Patents, Contracts, Petroleum-related, and Business. Prospective translators should have native-level capability, experience, technical knowledge, WP6.0 and a fax machine. **Calderon** maintains 2 in-house and several hundred outside translators in its pool.

Carolina Polyglot, Inc., PO Box 36334, Charlotte, NC 28236 Phone:(704)366-5781 Fax:(704)364-2998 e-mail: wmdepaula@aol.com Contact: Dr. William DePaula
Company founded 1971. Member: ATA, CATI. Accepts unsolicited resumes. Resumes are filed by language pair. E-mail and fax filed electronically. Requirements for applicants include academic degree, previous experience, professional affiliation/accreditation, references. Main languages (both ways) are French, Spanish, Italian, Portuguese, Romanian, German, Dutch, Arabic, Chinese, Vietnamese, and Japanese. Also translates Turkish, Farsi, Africaans, Hindi, Danish, Norwegian, Swedish, and Finnish. Main subjects are immigration, education, law, business, medicine, insurance, theology, ecology, literature, and computers. Uses over 30 translators. Owner is a distinguished former UN linguist.

Carolina Translation Service, Inc., 1431 Sterling Rd., Charlotte, NC 28209 Phone: (704)375-5267

Cato Research, Ltd., 4364 South Alston Ave., Ste. 201, Durham, NC 27713-2280 Phone: (919)361-2286 Fax: (919)361-2290 Web site: cato. com Contact: Cathy Worcester
Does not accept unsolicited resumes.

Center for Applied Linguistics, 4646 40th St. NW, Washington, DC 20016 Phone:(202)362-0700 Fax:(202)362-3740 e-mail: trans@cal.org Web site: cal.org/public/service/translat.htm Contact: Dr. James W. Stone, Director
Founded 1959. Member: ATA, NCATA. Uses freelance translators and interpreters. Accepts unsolicited resumes. Resumes entered in database. Translates all language pairs. Specialty in South Asian languages (Hindi, Urdu, Bengali, etc.) Handles material in all areas. Prospective translators are entered in database of available workers.CAL maintains a pool of 1,000 translators. It is a private, not-for-profit organization applying research and culture to educational, cultural, and social concerns. It issues dozens of publications annually, many in or including foreign languages. Services are available to the public through the translation services section of the company.

Center for Professional Advancement *See* **The Language Center**

Century International Communication, 1080 Saratoga Ave., Ste. 4, San Jose, CA 95129 Phone: (408)249-0452 Fax: (408)984-2341 Contact: M. Wood, Project Manager
Founded 1977. Translates all languages, all subjects. Prospective translators should submit a resume, letter of

recommendation, and a sample translation. Resumes are placed in a database depending on expertise and specialty area. **Century** maintains a pool of some 300 translators. The company is a division of Century School of Languages, Inc. Its services include desktop publishing.

Certified Interpreters & Translators (CIT), PO Box 390006, San Diego, CA 92149 Phone: (619)475-8586 Fax: (619)472-2157

Company founded 1983. Uses freelance translators and interpreters. Accepts unsolicited resumes. Resumes are filed by language and geographical area. Interpreters have to be certified. Main language pair is English-Spanish, followed by English into German and Tagalog, Russian, Arabic, and Japanese into English. Also Portuguese, Polish, and Vietnamese into English. Main subjects are legal, medical, technical, literary, commercial, as well as manuals. Does conference interpreting. Also does translator and interpreter training.

Chicago Multi-Lingua Graphics, Inc., 960 Grove St., Evanston, IL 60201 Phone: (847)864-3230 Fax: (847)864-3202 toll-free: 1-800-747-6047 e-mail: info@multimedia.com Contact: Yi Han Member: ATA

Community Interpreter Services, Catholic Charities/Greater Boston, 270 Washington St., Somerville, MA 02143 Phone: (617)629-5767 Fax: (617)629-5768 Contact: Lauren Gilman, Program Coordinator

Founded in 1986. Translates (both ways) Spanish, Haitian Creole, Cape Verdean Creole, Vietnamese, Russian, Khmer, French, Portuguese, Chinese, and Arabic. Also Italian, German, Somali, Bosnian, and Korean. Emphasis on Personal Document translation. Prospective translators should live in Massachusetts or a bordering state, and possess at least a Bachelor's degree, past translating experience, and fluency in at least two languages. Qualified resumes are responded to with an interview appointment. **CIS** maintains a pool of 250 translators and interpreters. They are a nonprofit service operated by Catholic Charities.

Counterpoint Language Consultants, Inc., PO Box 6184 Bridgewater, NJ 08807 Phone: (908)231-0991 Fax: (908)231-8266 e-mail: ctpt@ctpt. com Neil Morazar, Manager Contact: Laura Boublis

Company uses freelance translators and interpreters. Accepts unsolicited resumes. Languages (both ways) include German, French, Spanish, Italian, and Swahili.

Cybertec, Inc., 153 West Westfield Ave., Roselle Park, NJ 07204-1816 Phone:(908)245-3305 Fax:(908)245-5434 e-mail: cybertec_inc @compu-serve.com Web site: cybertecusa.com Contact: Joseph Nunes, President

Founded 1990. Member: ATA, NYCT. Uses freelance translators and interpreters. Accepts unsolicited resumes. Resumes are filed by language and specialty. Translators are required to have native ability in target language, and have at least one specialized field. Accreditation and/or diploma preferred. Translates all languages. Does over 5 million words per year. Over 100 translators in company's pool.

-D-

DI Media Services, Inc. 3408 NE 65th St., Ste. 200, Seattle, WA 98115 Phone:(206)525-9591 Fax:(206)525-9602 e-mail: mfleming@docint.com Web site: docint.com Contact: Michelle Fleming, President Deirdre Cleere, Localization Coordinator

Founded 1989. Member: ATA, NOTIS. Uses freelance translators and interpreters. Translates Spanish, French, German, Chinese, Russian, Japanese, Korean, and Portuguese, both from and into English, as well as various Asian languages. Emphasis on Software, Medical, Engineering, Legal, Business and Advertising translation. Prospective translators should provide their rates, three references, a sample translation, a summary of their experience, and their specialty. Must have ATA accreditation, 5 years experience in the field, 3 years translation experience. Resumes are sent to the president and processed by the translation coordinator; forms are then sent and the translator entered into the database. **Documents International** maintains a pool of 400 translators. The company also provides typesetting, graphic design, localization and multimedia services.

Dial-an-Interpreter, PO Box 27901-358, San Francisco, CA 94127 Phone:(415)682-TALK Fax:(415)682-8250 e-mail: dialectseix @network. com Web site: dial-an-interpreter.com Yancy C. Mendoza, Owner Contact: Garry A. Moss

Founded 1978. Uses freelance translators and interpreters. Accepts unsolicited resumes. Resumes are reviewed and filed for one year. Emphasis on Legal, Medical, and high-tech translation. Resumes are reviewed and filed. **Dial-an-Interpreter** maintains a pool of 350 translators. It is a full-service interpretation and translation agency.

Documents International, Inc., *see* **DI Media Services, Inc.**

Domenech & Associates, 5401 South Hyde Park Blvd., #805, Chicago, IL 60615 Phone: (312)684-2949

-E-

East West Institute, 110 North Berendo St., Los Angeles, CA 90004 Phone: (213)389-9050 Fax: (213)382-0757 e-mail: ewincc@mindspring. com Contact: Personnel Manager

Company founded 1989. Uses freelance translators and interpreters. Accepts unsolicited resumes. Translates all languages, both from and into English. Prospective translators should be U.S. residents. Resumes are kept and applicants called if necessary. Interpreters provided only in Southern California.

East-West Concepts, Inc., PO Box 527, Kalaheo, HI 96741 Phone: (808) 332-5220 Fax:(808)332-5531 e-mail: janoss@aol.com Janos Samu, President Contact: Judy Roberts, Translation Coordinator

Founded 1989. Member: ATA, NYAS, ADPA. Uses freelance translators and interpreters. Accepts unsolicted resumes. Resumes are evaluated and entered in database. If rates are reasonable, applicant is given a short assignment and receives feedback. Translates (both ways) Hungarian, Czech, Albanian, Bulgarian, Polish, Russian, Greek, as well as Turkish, Slovak, Slovene, Urdu, Georgian, Armenian, Estonian, and 70 other languages. Emphasis on Business, Technical, Computer, Scientific, Legal, Advertising, Military and Social Work translation. **East-West** translates 3-4 million words per year, and maintains a pool of 2684 translators. While company has its strongest profile in Eastern European and Baltic languages, it became also strong in the languages of the Pacific area and Asia. Handles primarily translation and DTP in 85 languages.

Eriksen Translations Inc., 32 Court St., 20th Fl., Brooklyn, NY 11201 Phone: (718)802-9010 Fax: (718)802-0041 e-mail: info@ erikseninc.com Web site: erikseninc.com Vigdis Eriksen, President Contact: Lisa Horan, Project Coordinator

Founded 1986. Member: ATA, NYCT, NCATI, Swedish Association of Professional Translators. Translates Danish, Finnish, Icelandic, Norwegian and Swedish, both from and into English. Emphasis on Computer, Legal, Financial, Advertising, Medical, Manuals, and Fine Arts translation. Resumes are evaluated and filed accordingly. **Eriksen** maintains an in-house staff of 15 translators. The company also provides editing and typesetting services and Web site development.

EuroNet Language Services, 295 Madison Ave., 45th Fl., New York, NY 10017 Phone:(212)271-0401 Fax:(212)271-0404 e-mail: euronet @mindspring.com Eleonore Speckens, President Contact: Anouk, HRM

Founded 1989. Member: NYCT, ATA. Uses freelance translators and interpreters. Accepts unsolicited resumes. Translates Spanish, French, Portuguese, Italian, Dutch, German, Swedish, and other Euro-pean languages, both from and into English. Translates all subjects. Prospective translators must be native speakers with bilingual capacity in English and possess a university degree. Resumes are reviewed and added to a database. **EuroNet** maintains a pool of 300 translators. The company does voice-overs.

Expert Translators, 11400 North Kendall Drive, Ste. 206, Miami, FL 33176 Phone:(305)279-0583 Fax:(305)273-4407 e-mail: xpert@bellsouth. net Web site: expert-translators.com Angela M. Greiffenstein, President Contact: Emily Correal, General Manager

Founded 1980. Member: South Dade Chamber of Commerce. Uses freelance translators and interpreters. Accept unsolicited resumes. Resumes are filed by language pairs. Requires 10 years experience and either ATA accreditation or translation degree. Translates (both ways) Spanish, Brazilian Portuguese, French, Italian, German, Russian, Dutch, and Greek. Translated about 8 million words a year. Maintains pool of 35 translators.

-F-

Flagg & Associates, 759 North Milwaukee St., Milwaukee, WI 53202 Phone: (414)278-8322 Fax: (414)964-0556 e-mail: gpflagg@yahoo.com Contact: Arnold Flagg

FLS, Inc., 3609 A-5 Memorial Parkway SW, Huntsville AL 35801 Phone: (205)881-1120 Fax: (205)880-1112 email: flstrans@aol.com Web site: flstranslation.com Contact: Judith H. Smith
Company founded 1979. Member: ATA. Uses freelance translators and inter-preters. Unsolicited resumes accepted.

*Foreign Language Center, Inc., *see* **OneWorld Language Solutions**

Foreign Language Graphics, 4303 North Figueroa St., Los Angeles, CA 90065 Phone: (213)224-8417

-G-

Geonexus Communications, 667 Lytton Ave., Palo Alto, CA 94301 Phone:(650)321-6545 Fax:(650)321-9398 e-mail: info@geonexus .com Web site: geonexus.com Contact: David Crankshaw
Founded 1992. Member: ATA, NCTA. Translates mainly (both ways) Japanese, French, German, Spanish, Italian, Chinese, Portuguese, Korean, Russian, and Swedish. Emphasis on technology, marketing, and training. Prospective trans-lators should have experience, appropriate hardware and software, business skills, sample translations. Resumes are reviewed, entered into files, acknowledged with response card. **Geonexus** maintains a pool of over 1000 translators. The company provides document translation, website and software localization, and interpretation in Silicon Valley.

Global Translations & Interpreters Services, Inc., 277 Wellington St. West, Ste. 710, Toronto, Ontario M5V 3E4 CANADA Phone: (416)593-1444 Fax: (416)593-6344 e-mail:mailbox@globaltranslation. com Contact: TIm Koresssis, Director
Founded 1972.Member: ATA, Board of Trade of Metropolitan Toronto. Uses freelance translators and interpreters. Accepts unsolicited resumes. Applicants should have a university-level education or its equivalent in both their source and target languages. Resumes should be faxed, mailed or e-mailed, after which they are kept on file until required. Translates (both ways) Spanish, Italian, Greek, Chinese, Vietnamese, and French. Emphasis on Legal, Medical, and Technical translation. **Global Translations** maintains a pool of 1500 translators. The company specializes in legal document translation and interpreting, as well as medical and insurance matters.

*Groupe Mistral, 522 Brewers Mill Rd., Harrodsburg, KY 40330 Phone: (606)366-4211 Fax:(606)366-4362 e-mail: groupmist @compu-serve.com Contact: Sylvie Gadness
Founded 1995. Translates French, Haitian Creole, Latvian, Russian, Romanian, Mandarin Chinese and Arabic, both from and into English, as well as Japanese, and Hungarian. Emphasis on Engineering, Financial, Medical and Advertising translation. The company does not work with freelance translators; it is rather a consortium of in-house personnel. Prospective translators should be local, within driving distance, and should have translation experience. **Groupe Mistral** maintains an in-house pool of 10 translators. The company specializes in French Computer translation.

-H-

HablEspaña Language Center, Inc., *see* **New England Translations**

Inlingua Translation Service, 95 Summit Ave., Summit, NJ 07901 Phone: (908)522-0622 Fax: (908)522-1433 e-mail: 104405.222 @compu-serve.com Deborah Hinckley, President Contact: Susan Baldani
Founded 1968. Uses freelance translators and interpreters. Accepts unsolicited resumes. Resumes are kept on file for future jobs. Applicants must have computer, fax, and modem. Ten top languages are Spanish, French, Italian, Portuguese, Russian, German, Chinese, Japanese, Danish, and Polish. Also translates Korean and Romanian. Main areas are licenses, birth certificates, and transcripts. Has pool of some 25 translators. Operates as language school with translation services.

Inter Lingua, Inc, 1711 East 15th St., Tulsa, OK 74104 Phone: (918)743-2424 Fax: (918)743-1347 email: ilinc@ionet@net Contact: Carolyn Quintero, President
Company founded 1983. Member: ATA, NAJIT. Offers translation and interpretation services in Spanish, Portuguese, German, Polish, Chinese and most other languages from and into English. **Inter Lingua** uses freelance translators and interpreters. Unsolicited resumes from freelancers are filed by language. Translation subjects oil and gas, advertising, manufacturing, quality assurance, and many others.

International Bureau of Translations, Inc, 10291 North Meridian St., Ste. 350, Indianapolis, IN 46290 Phone: ((317)581-0060 Fax: (317) 581-1160 e-mail: ibt-inc@iei.com Contact: Christian Gecewicz, CEO

Founded 1976. Member: OTIAQ, Indianapolis Chamber of Commerce, IUPUI, Indian University. Translates French, Spanish, German, Portuguese, Dutch, Italian, Japanese, Chinese, Korean and Russian, both from and into English, as well as various Slavic, Scandinavian, Eastern European and Asian languages. Emphasis on Business Correspondence, Medical, Technical, Legal and Personal Document translation. Prospective translators should be native speakers with access to a computer, modem, or fax. They should send a rate chart with their resume. Resumes are filed and the translator contacted as the need arises. **IBT** maintains a pool of 150 translators. The company does foreign videos, court interpretation, cultural presentations, and conducts language classes. They research the cultural acceptability of company names, product names and slogans, and are the official translators for the International Violin Competition.

International Effectiveness Centers, 690 Market St., Ste. 700, San Francisco, CA 94104 Phone:(415)788-4149 Fax:(415)788-4829 e-mail: iec@ie-center.com Contact: Taryk Rouchdy, CEO
Founded 1972. Member: ATA, NCTA. Translates Spanish, Chinese, Russian, and Portuguese, both from and into English, French and Vietnamese from English, and Japanese into English. Emphasis on Legal, Technical and Children's Book translation. Uses freelance translators and interpreters. Accept unsolicited resumes. Prospective translators must have at least 3 years experience and be tested unless they hold current ATA accreditation. Resumes are screened for qualifications and appropriate equipment and, if qualified, entered into a data base **IEC** maintains a pool of 7000 translators in its data base, 170 of whom are used regularly. The company also does desktop publishing in all languages, as well as voice-overs, dubbing, promotional work, cross-cultural and language training, and international business consulting.

International Language Source, Inc., PO Box 338, Holland, OH 43528-0338 Phone:(419)865-4374 Fax:(419)865-7725 e-mail: ilsource @worldnet.att.net Contact: Ryan Stevens, Account Manager
Founded 1981. Member: TAITA, Toledo Area Chamber of Commerce. Uses freelance translators and interpreters. Accepts unsolicited resumes. Prospective translators should have a specialty area and the appropriate resources for projects in that area. Resumes are kept for 6 months in an active database. Contact may involve the paid translation of a short sample. Translates Spanish, French, German, Russian and Korean, both from and into English, and Japanese, Chinese, Portuguese, Italian and Polish from English. Emphasis on Glass Manufacturing and Retail, Automotive OEM and Aftermarket, Furniture, Legal, Industrial and Healthcare translation. In addition to translation services, **ILS** provides video and interactive CD-ROM translation and voiceovers. The company is willing to consider internships and cooperative projects with other translation companies.

International School of Languages (ISL), 9581 W. Pico Blvd., Los Angeles, CA 90035 Phone: (310)557-1711 Fax: (310)550-0601 e-mail: english@bhisl.com Web site: bhisl.com Henry H. Mochizuki,

General Director Contact: Iva Mavrovich, Admissions/Translations
Founded in 1955. Member: Council for Private Postsecondary Vocational Education; Beverly Hills Chamber of Commerce. Translates (both ways) Spanish, French, Mandarin Chinese, Japanese, and Italian. Also German, Portuguese, Arabic, and Hebrew. Emphasis on Technical Manual, Medical and Personal Document translation. Prospective translators should have at least a B.A. and experience; the company employs only native speakers. Resumes are reviewed by the general director, who then calls qualified candidates for interviews. ISL maintains a pool of 100 translators. The company also provides voice-overs for the film industry and teaches English as a Second Language, both in groups and privately, and provides private lessons in all other languages.

International Translating Bureau, 16125 West 12 Mile Rd., South-field, MI 48076-2912 Phone:(248)559-1677 Fax:(248)559-1679 e-mail: itbinc @itbtranslations.com Contact: Mariano Pallarés, President
Founded 1977. Translates all language pairs. Emphasis on Automotive, Engineer-ing, Machine Tool, Legal, Medical, and Public Relations translation. Prospective translators should be native speakers of the target language, have at least 5 years residence in the source-language country, and have academic training or on-job experience in a specialized field. Candidates must have computer, fax and current software, particularly WordPerfect and Word for Windows for PC or Mac. Resumes are scanned for qualifications in which the company is interested and filed for future use. ITB maintains a pool of 250 translators. The company offers accurate, native-like translations.

The International Word, 7117 Farnam St., Ste. 21, Omaha, NE 98132 Phone: (402)393-2888 Fax: (402)393-2801 e-mail: 73122.3507 @compu-serve.com, tiw@aol.com Contact: Ralf Weber

Intex Translations, 9021 Melrose Ave., Ste. 205, W. Hollywood, CA 90069 Phone:(310)275-9571

Fax:(310)271-1319 e-mail: intex@intextrans. com Web site: intextrans.com Contact: Mrs. L. Manouche Ragsdale, President Contact: Luke Collins (resumes) Birgita Farr (production)
Founded 1981. Member: ATA, SCATIA, FACC, US-Mexico Chamber of Commerce. Uses freelance translators and interpreters. Accepts unsolicited resumes. Requires degree and 5 years experience. Translates all languages. Emphasis on cosmetics, advertising, legal subjects, and entertainment. Does conference and business interpreting. Resumes are reviewed and analyzed, and a select number are sent application packets. Intex maintains a pool of 450+ translators.

IRCO/International Language Bank, 1336 East Burnside St., Portland, OR 97214 Phone: (503)234-0068 Fax: (503)233-4724 e-mail: ilb@europa.com Web site: irco.org Contact: Translation Services Super-visor
Founded 1976. Member: ATA, NOTIS. Uses freelance translators. Accepts unsolicited resumes. Applicants should have a degree in language and literature, science, etc. Should own PC or Mac, fax machine and e-mail, and have experience with the Internet and desktop publishing. Resumes are sorted by language and applicant's last name and filed for future use. Translates Spanish, Russian, Romanian, Serbo-Croatian Vietnamese, Cambodian, Laotian, Mien, Hmong, Chinese, Japanese, Amharic, Tigrinya, Creole and Thai, all from English. Emphasis on community translation projects, such as government forms, employee manuals, social service literature, and translation for refugee and immigrant communities in the U.S. ILB maintains a pool of 100+ translators. They specialize in refugee-related documents and languages. IRCO is the International Refugees Center of Oregon and is a nonprofit agency. ILB has grown from providing language services to refugee communities to a full-service translation and interpreting agency.

IRU (International Resources Unlimited), 2909 Hillcroft Ave., Ste. 538, Houston, TX 77057 Phone: (713)266-0020 Fax: (713)266-1716 e-mail: IRU2000@aol.com Web site: home.aol.com.iru2000 Contact: Ms. Elke Krause, Director
Founded 1989. Member: ATA, HITA. Translates Spanish, French and German, both from and into English, and Chinese, Italian and Russian into English. Emphasis on Engineering, Humanities, Educational, Oil & Gas, Legal, and General translation. Prospective translators should have prior experience and excellent computer literacy, as well as the ability to deliver in a timely manner. Resumes are reviewed and entered into a data base by language. IRU maintains a pool of ±200 translators. The company also provides language classes, chaperon services and cross-cultural seminars,

with emphasis on Spanish and German.

Iverson Language Associates, Inc., P.O. Box 511759, Milwaukee, WI 53203 Phone:(414)271-1144 Fax:(414)271-0144 e-mail: info@ iversonlang.com Web site: iversonlang.com Contact: Steven P. Iverson, President

Founded 1986. Member: STC. Translates French, Spanish, Japanese, Italian, Arabic, Dutch, and Korean from English, and Portuguese, German, Polish, Chinese and all other languages, both from and into English. Emphasis on Technical Manuals (large machines), Medical Operators' Manuals, Spec Sheets, Financial, Software, Advertising Packaging, and Legal translations. Prospective translators should have computer, fax, current software, e-mail. Must be native speakers in the target language, with a technical background and formal training in a specific field of concentration. Three years experience in the industry and good writing skills are preferred. Resumes are reviewed internally for the required criteria. If so, they are sent a Translator Profile to fill out, and the completed form made available to project managers for use on new projects. **Iverson** maintains a pool of 600 translators. The company provides translation, interpretation, typesetting and video narration services in most major languages, as well as technical writing and illustration. Typesetting capabilities include Chinese and Japanese.

-J-

Japan Pacific Publications, Inc., 419 Occidental Ave. S. #509, Seattle, WA 98104 Phone: (206)622-7443 Fax: (206)621-1786 email: japanpac @halcyon.com Web site: Japan Pacific.com Contact: Mr. Andrew Taylor, President

Founded 1983. Member: ATA. Uses freelance translators and interpreters. Accepts unsolicited resumes. Resumes are entered into database and evaluated for skills and experience. Main language is Japanese. Also translates Chinese and Korean. Maintains pool of 35 translators. Translation, DTP, pre-press, image setting.

-K-

Korean Technical Communications, *see* **Transcend Languages, Inc.**

-L-

LangTech International, 5625 SW 170th Ave., Aloha, OR 97007-3320 Phone: (503)646-2478 e-mail: LangTech@class.oregonvos.net Web site: latco.org/ langtech.htm Contact: Douglas Foran, Owner

Founded 1994. Member: Latin American Trade Council of Oregon. Translates French (European and Canadian), Spanish, Italian and Portuguese (Brazilian and Lusitanian), both from and into English. Emphasis on Scientific/ Technical, Mechanical, Electronics, Automotive, Agricultural, Legal, Health Care/Medical and Employee Relations translation. Also interpretation and audio/visual narration.

Language Associates, 4924 N. Miller, Oklahoma City, OK 73112 Phone: (405)946-1624 Fax: (405)946-1302 e-mail: cessyevans@aol.com Contact: Cecilia Evans, General Manager

Founded 1980. Member: ATA, NAJIT. Uses freelance translators and interpreters. Accepts unsolicited resumes. Resumes are entered in the system for future reference. Main languages (both ways) are Spanish, French, German, Russian, Japanese, and Korean. Also translates Chinese, Italian, Portuguese, Arabic, and more.

The Language Bank, 875 O'Farrell St., Ste. 105, San Francisco, CA 94109 Phone: (415)885-0827 Fax: (415)885-1304 Contact: Yen Nguyen-le, Manager

Founded 1987. Uses freelance translators and interpreters. Accepts unsolicited resumes. Resumes are screened for qualifications. Main languages are Spanish, Chinese, Vietnamese, Russian, Tagalog, Thai, Laotian, Cambodian, and French. Emphasis on social services. Pool of more than 100 translators.

The Language Center, 144 Tices Ln., E. Brunswick, NJ 08816 Phone: (732)613-4554 Fax: (732)238-7659 e-mail: tlc@thelanguagectr.com Web site: thelanguagectr.com Contact: Jim Kish Member:ATA.

The Language Center Inc., 7 Gilliam Ln., Riverside, CT 06878-0520 Phone: (203)698-1907 Fax:(203)698-2043 e-mail: thelanguagecenterinc @worldnet.att.net Contact: Siri Ostensen, President
Founded 1978. Translates (both ways) Spanish, French, German, Portuguese, all Scandinavian languages, Italian, Japanese, Chinese, and Russian. Emphasis on Technical, Commercial and Legal translation. Prospective translators should provide sample translations. Resumes are entered into a data base. **The Language Center** maintains a pool of 30 translators.

The Language Center, Inc., 313 6th Ave., Ste. 400, Pittsburgh, PA 15222 Phone: (412)261-1101 Fax: (216)261-1159 Contact: Mr. Leslie A. Dutka

The Language Company, PO Box 42376, Houston, TX 77042-2940 Phone: (713)952-6704 Fax:(713)952-5513 e-mail: 105361.1072 @compu serve.com Contact: Danielle Y. Pung, President
Founded 1981. Member: ATA, AATIA, HITA. Uses freelance translators and interpreters. Accepts unsolicited resumes. Translates French, Spanish, Russian, German, Portuguese, etc., both from and into English. Emphasis on Technical, Patent and Legal translation. Potential translators should have word processing and transmission capabilities. Resumes are reviewed and filed.

Language Company Translations, P.O. Box 1396, Norman, OK 73070 Phone: (405)321-5380 Fax: (405)366-7242 e-mail: 71564.2044 @compu-serve.com Contact: Nancy T. Hancock, Director
Founded 1982. Member: ATA. Translates all languages in all technical disciplines. Potential translators should have experience and total fluency. They should be able to produce translations on disk if needed. Resumes are acknowledged and filed. Freelancers are contacted when appropriate work comes in. **Language Company Translations** maintains a pool of 40 translators. The company can take materials through final printing, working with commercial printers and supervising production. They also accept resumes from freelance interpreters.

The Language Connection, PO Box 1962, Laguna Beach, CA 92652 Phone: (949)497-9393 Fax: (949)497-7515 e-mail: 102513.1774 @compuserve.com Web site: languageconnection.com Contact: J. Arturo Valdivia, President Member: ATA

Language Dynamics, 931 Howe Ave. #107, Sacramento, CA 95825-3908 Phone: (916)920-4062 Fax: (916)920-3594 Web site: langdyna.com Contact: Rhody, Manager
Founded 1979. Translates Spanish, French, Chinese, German, Italian, Japanese, Russian and Hmong, both from and into English. All subject areas are translated. Prospective translators should be of high quality. Resumes are read and kept on file for contact on an as-needed basis.

Language Intelligence, Ltd., 16 North Goodman St., Rochester, NY 14607 Phone: (716)244-5578 Fax: (716)244-7880 e-mail: mail@lan-guageintelligence.com Contact: Irene White, President
Founded 1988. Member: ATA, STC. Main languages (both ways) are Italian, Portuguese, Spanish, Chinese, Japanese, Swedish, Norwegian, Danish, and Dutch. Emphasis on Technical Manual and Documentation translation. Prospective translators should have a BA degree or equivalent experience and be native speakers of the target language. Resumes are reviewed and the applicants contacted if they match with the needs of the company. **Language Intelligence** maintains a pool of about 30 translators. The company provides high-volume localization for software, video and documentation.

Language Learning Enterprises (LLE), 1100 17th St. NW, Ste. 900, Washington, DC 20036 Phone: (202)775-0444 Fax: (202)785-5584 e-mail: lang-lrn@lle-inc.com Web site: lle-inc.com Kathleen Diamond Contact: Attn: Linguistic Resources
Founded 1979. Resumes are carefully screened; prospective translators and interpreters are then interviewed over phone, references checked, and then tried out on a small project first. Requires minimum 2 years experience. Translates all languages "from Arabic to Zulu," both from and into English. Emphasis in all technical areas, with a specialty in medical interpretation. **LLE** maintains a pool of 12 full-time people with 1000 linguists on call. The company is the creator of LLE-Link, a 24-hour-a-day, 365 days-a-year telephone interpretation service using conference calling.

Language Link Corporation, 3100 Broadway, Ste. 110, Kansas City, MO 64111 Phone: (816)753-3122 Fax: (816)753-3262 e-mail: 72734.140@compuserve.com Contact: Mrs. Anne L. Burkart Member: ATA. Uses freelance translators and interpreters. Accpts unsolicited resumes. Does over 50 languages in all areas.

The Language School - Translation Service, *see* **TLS - Translation Service**

The Language Service, Inc., 806 Main St., Poughkeepsie, NY 12603 Phone: (914)473-4303 Fax:(914)473-4467 e-mail: info@tlsmedtrans.com Web site: tlsmedtrans.com Henry Fischbach, Owner Contact: Jeanne De Tar
Founded 1950. Member: ATA, FIT. Uses freelance translators and interpreters. Accepts unsolicited resumes. Qualified linguists are filed for future reference. Main languages (both ways) are German, French, Spanish, Italian, and Portuguese, and Japanese into English. Also Dutch and Swedish into English. Main areas are medical, legal, environmental. Does about one million words a year. Works with various translators, but mainly with a steady group of about ten. Owner is co-founder and former president of the ATA.

Language Services Associates, Inc., 607 North Easton, C, PO Box 205, Willow Grove, PA 19090 Phone: (215)657-6571 Fax: (215)659-7210 e-mail: lsa@call-lsa.com Laura K.T. Schriver, company head Contact: Christina Murphy
Founded 1991. Member: ATA, DVTA, NAJIT, CHICATA, NOTA. Uses freelance translators and interpreters. Accepts unsolicited resumes. Resumes are acknowledged, kept, and used when needed. Applicants should have ATA accreditation. Main languages (both ways) are Spanish, German, French, Chinese, Japanese, Korean, Vietnamese, Russian, Hindi, Italian, and Tamil. Also Cambodian, Arabic, Farsi, Hebrew, Dutch and more. Emphasis on Legal and corporate translation. **Language Services Associates** maintains a pool of 745 translators.

Liaison Language Center, 3500 Oak Lawn Ave., Ste. 110 LB 32, Dallas, TX 75219-4343 Phone: (214)528-2731 Fax: (214)522-7167 e-mail: liaison@liaisonlanguage.com Web site: liaisonlanguage.com Contact: Gerda Stendell
Founded 1968. Member: ATA, Chamber of Commerce. Uses freelance translators and interpreters. Accepts unsolicited resumes. Translated all languages and all subjects. Has a pool of around 500 active translators.

Linguistic Systems, Inc., 130 Bishop Allen Drive, Cambridge, MA 02139 Phone:(617)864-3900 Fax:(617)864-5186 e-mail: info@linguist. com Web site: linguist.com Contact: Martin Roberts, President
Founded 1967. Member: ATA. Uses freelance translators and interpreters. Accepts unsolicited resumes. Applicants should have relevant education and experience. Translates (both ways) mainly Arabic, Chinese, French, German, Italian, Japanese, Korean, Portuguese, Russian, and Spanish, as well as all other languages. Emphasis on Technical translation. **LSI** maintains a pool of about 4000 translators, and translates about 10 million words a year. The company provides translation, interpretation, voiceover, and machine translation editing services.

-M-

M/C International, 16675 West Park Circle Drive, Chagrin Falls, OH 44023 Phone:(216)543-5168 Fax:(216)543-4084 e-mail: mcinternational @stratos.net or scottyline@aol.net Harry Cunningham, President Contact: Peggy L. Mares, Office Manager / Chris Davis, Production Manager
Founded 1969. Translates Spanish, French, German, Italian, Portuguese, Russian, Chinese (Mandarin), Japanese, Arabic, Dutch, Hungarian, Korean and Norwegian, both from and into English. Emphasis on Technical Manuals, Instruction Booklets, Legal, Advertising Literature, Medical and Scientific Literature translations and Video Presentations, Computer Technology and Programming. Pro-spective translators should have a college degree, be computer literate, and have a computer, fax, and e-mail capabilities. Resumes are reviewed and filed, and if qualified, a request for references and a test exercise are sent. **M/C** maintains a pool of 50 translators. The company is a full-service translation bureau. It also provides 4-color printing services, desktop publishing and typesetting, both to clients and to other translators. In addition, they operate their own travel agency.

M² Ltd., 9210 Wightman Rd., Montgomery Village, MD 20886 Phone: (301)977-4281 Fax: (301)926-5046 e-mail: info@m2ltd.com Web site: m2ltd.com Mercedes Pellet, President Contact: Paul Henning, Sales Manager

Founded 1979. Member: ATA, Society for Technical Communication, American Management Assn. uses freelance translators and interpreters. Accepts unsolicited resumes. Applicants should be native speakers of the target language, with 2-5 years minimum experience, and should be able to provide samples and references. Resumes are responded to with a "Subcontractor Profile." Completed profiles are reviewed, and qualified applicants are added to a database. Translates French, Italian, German, Japanese, Chinese, Swedish, Portuguese, Arabic, Russian, Hungarian, Flemish, Thai and Dutch from English, and Spanish into English. Emphasis on Computer Software, Electronics, Engineering, Medical, Legal, Corporate Marketing and Office Equipment translation. The company does not provide interpreting services. M² maintains a pool of 1,000 translators. The company has become a specialist in the localization of computer-based equipment and software, and is heavily involved in software development, training, and adaptation of English-language materials for use in other cultures and languages. In addition to translators, the company is interested in proofreaders and editors in all languages.

Marion J. Rosley Secretarial, Transcription & Translation Services, 41 Topland Rd., Hartsdale, NY 10530 Phone: (914)682-9718 Fax: (914) 761-1384 e-mail: mrosley@rosley.com Web site: rosley.com Contact: Marion J. Rosley, President

Founded 1977. Member: NYCT, World Trade Council of Westchester, Connecticut Foreign Trade Assn., Westconn. Translates all languages. Emphasis on Legal, Medical, Technical, and Business Correspondence translation. The company provides interpreting services in all languages. Prospective translators should have excellent skills and reasonable prices. Resumes are filed for future use. **Rosley Services** maintains a pool of "hundreds" of translators. The company provides secretarial, transcription and translation services, including cassette transcription of conferences.

MasterWord Services, Inc., 303 Stafford, Ste. 204, Houston, TX 77079 Phone:(713)589-0810 Fax:(713)589-1104 e-mail: masterword@ masterword.com Web site: masterword.com Ludmila Rusakova, Pres-ident Contact: Jennifer Kramer

Founded 1993. Member: ATA, Azeri Translators Association. Translates Russian, Spanish, Azeri, Brazilian Portuguese and Chinese, both from and into English. Emphasis on Oil and Gas, Drilling, Legal and Medical translations. Prospective translators should have significant translation experience, especially in the oil/gas or legal areas, and show quality performance on the company's certification exam. All resumes are acknowledged, and after prescreening, ap-proximately 10% are sent an in-house certification exam, primarily in Russian or Spanish. They are then phoned for an in-person interview. **MasterWord** maintains a pool of 35-50 translators. The company also has offices in Baku, Azerbaijan, and is involved in ongoing projects in Europe, South America and Asia.They also have affiliates in Washington, DC, New York, London and Moscow.

Metropolitan Interpreters and Translators Worldwide, Inc., 110 E. 42nd St., Ste. 802, New York, NY 10017 Phone: (212)986-5050 Fax: (212)983-5998 e-mail: metlang@aol.com Web site: metlang.com Irene Ehrlich, Head Contact: Human Resources Mgr.

Founded 1990. Member: ATA, NYCT, NAJIT, IAFL. Uses freelance translators and interpreters. Accept unsolicited resumes. Resumes are entered in a database. Translates all languages. Emphasis on legal and law enforcement. About 500 in translator pool.

-N-

NCS Enterprises, Inc., 702 Copeland St., #11, Pittsburgh PA 15232 Phone: (412)682-3422 Fax: (412)682-3121 e-mail: snagy@ncs-pubs.com Web site: ncs-pubs.com Contact: Charlene Nagy, President Contact: Stephanie Nagy

Founded 1992. Member: ATA. Uses freelance translators and interpreters. Accepts unsolicited resumes. All resume are reviewed and entered into database.

New England Translations, 71 Summer St., 5th Fl., Boston, MA 02110 Phone: (617)426-4868 Fax: (617)695-9349 e-mail: netranslations@ langcenters.com Web site:langcenters.com Contact: Ken Krall, Director
Founded 1986. Member: ATA. Uses freelance translators and interpreters. Accepts unsolicited resumes. Resumes are entered into databse by language and specialty. Requires experience. Translates Spanish, Portuguese, French, German, Italian, Chinese, Vietnamese, Korean and Japanese from English, and Spanish into English. Emphasis on Finance, Legal, Marketing, Industrial and Medical trans-lation, with specialties in Financial and Medical. Prospective translators should have PC or Mac, fax, modem. A small sample translation should be sent with the resume. Resumes are entered into a database by language pair and technical specialty after qualifications are reviewed. **NET** maintains a pool of 800 translators. The company is dedicated to the translation of all major languages. It also provides instruction in Spanish only.

-O-

Okada & Sellin Translations, LLC 1950 Addison St., Ste. 101, Berkeley CA 94704 Phone: (510)803-9896 Fax: (510)843-5603 e-mail: okada@ostrans.com Web site: ostrans.com Contact: Hiromi Okada or Robert G. Sellin
Founded 1996. Member: ATA, STC. Uses freelance translators and interpreters. Accepts unsolicited resumes. Resumes are reviewed and graded. Work sample are welcome. Requires e-mail. Translates all major Asian and European languages. Focuses on patents and other technical, scientific, pharma/biotech, and legal subjects. Does around 10 million words a year.

OneWorld Language Solutions, 2909 Cole Ave., Ste. 300, Dallas, TX 75204 Phone: (214)871-2909 Fax: (214)871-1945 e-mail: ghayes@one-worldlanguage Web site: oneworldlanguage.com Contact: Gabriele Hayes, Director
Founded 1990. Member: ATA, META. Uses freelance translators and interpreters. Accepts unsolicited resumes. Requires experience, prefers ATA members. Resumes are entered in database and applicants are contacted when the need arises. Translates (both ways) mainly Spanish, French, German, Italian, and Russian. Also Japanese, Dutch, and Chinese. Provides interpretation and language training. Maintains a pool of over 400 translators.

-P-

P.H. Brink International, 6100 Golden Valley Rd., Minneapolis, MN 55422 Phone:(612)591-1977 Fax:(612)542-9138 e-mail: info@phbrink. com Web site: phbrink.com Paul Brink, President Contact: Greg Brink
Member: ATA. Uses freelance translators and interpreters. Accepts unsolicited resumes. Resumes are screened and best ones are called for test. Requires college degree and native speaking ability. Translates mainly English into major European languages and Japanese. Subjects are mostly technical. Employs 150 full-time translators.

Pacolet International Translation Co., 11405 Main St., Roscoe IL 61073 Phone: (815)623-1608 Fax: (815)623-1907 e-mail: pacolet@inwave.com Web site: pacolet.com Contact: Julie Johnson McKee, President
Founded 1993. Member: ATA, Greater Rockford Chamber of Commerce. Uses freelance translators and interpreters. Accepts unsolicited resumes. Resumes are reviewed for language skills and specialties, and entered in database. ATA affiliation or translation degree required. Strong professional experience preferred. Translates mainly Spanish, French, Dutch, Italian, Portuguese, Swedish, Finnish, Chinese, Japanese, and Korean. Also other European and Asian languages, Arabic and Farsi. Emphasis on technical subjects, heavy equipment, engines, aerospace, food service equipment, business contracts and proposals. Maintains a pool of 300 translators. Did one millions dollars worth of translation in 1988. Strong background in marketing communications and broadcasting. Company is family-friendly and develops long-term "partnerships" (company-translator-customer are a team).

Para-Plus Translations, Inc., PO Box 92, Barrington, NJ 08007 Phone: (609)547-3695 Fax:(609)547-3345 e-mail: paraplus@erols.com Web site: para-plus.com Contact: Sonia Santiago, President
Founded 1981. Member: DVTA, NAJIT, ATA. Translates Spanish, German, French, Creole, Chinese, Japanese, Korean, Italian, Russian, Vietnamese, Arabic and Korean, both from and into English. Emphasis on Legal, Medical, Pharmaceutical and Technical translation. Prospective translators must be native speakers, college graduates, and have areas of special expertise. Candidates should submit a list of equipment available to them, as well as a sample of their work. Resumes are reviewed and a follow-up letter sent in response. **Para-Plus** maintains a pool of approximately 95 translators. The company also provides interpretation services in over 75 language and foreign-language tape translations and transcriptions

Peters Translation, *see* **PTIGlobal**

Professional Advancement Enterprises, 2182 Saginaw SE, Grand Rapids, MI 49506 Phone: (616)956-9443, (800)421-1943 Fax: (616) 956-7973 Web site: paeworld.com Contact: Jorge Garcia

ProTrans, Inc., P.O.Box 507, Barrington, RI 02806 Phone: (401)245-9535 Fax: (401)245-9534 e-mail: protrans@ids.net Web site: protrans1. com Contact: H. Karin Weldy
Founded 1989. Member: ATA, NETA, Greater Providence Chamber of Commerce, WACRI. Uses freelance translators. Accepts unsolicited resumes. Applicants should provide sample translations, references, work history; they need to be *full-time* translators. Resumes usually result in contact to ask questions, determine fees and check references. Main languages are English into Spanish, Portuguese, French, German, Italian, Japanese, Chinese, and Swedish. Also German, Dutch into English, and English into Cambodian and Laotian. Emphasis on technical manuals, automotive, legal, ad copy, educational, brochures, and catalogs. Maintains a pool of about 350 translators.

PTIGlobal, 9900 SW Wilshire, Ste. 280, Portland, OR 97225 Phone:(503)297-2165 Fax:(503)297-0655 e-mail: global@petrans.com Web site: petrans.com or ptiglobal.com Mollie Peters, Head Contact: Lea Fields
Founded 1977. Member: ATA. Uses freelance translators and interpreters. Accepts unsolicited resumes. Resumes are reviewed, graded, and kept in database. Requires FrameMaker; Trados helpful. Main subjects are technical, software, and web applications.

-R-

Rennert Bilingual Translation Group, 216 East 45th St., New York, NY 10025 Phone:(212)867-8700 Fax:(212)867-7666 e-mail: translations @rennert.com Web site: rennert.com Contact: Mikael Poulsen, Director
Founded 1973. Member: ATA, New York Circle of Translators. Translates Spanish, German, French, Japanese, Portuguese, Italian, Chinese, Turkish, Swedish, Russian, Korean, and most other languages, both from and into English. Emphasis on all aspects of Patent Law, Marketing, Public Relations, Business and Finance, Videos and Educational Material translation. Prospective translators should possess training and experience in the specific fields. Resumes are reviewed for education and experience, and a Rennert application is sent to the translator for completion. **Rennert** maintains a pool of 1500 translators. The company specializes in translation for legal, business and corporate clients.

-S-

Sally Low and Associates, 600 West Santa Ana Blvd., Ste. #208, Santa Ana, CA 92701 Phone: (714)834-9032 Fax: (714)834-9035 e-mail: slasehadla@aol.com Contact: Lisa Alvarez Member: ATA

Schreiber Translations, Inc. (STI), 51 Monroe St., Ste. 101, Rockville, MD 20850 Phone:(301)424-7377 Fax:(301)424-2336 e-mail: translation@schreibernet.com Web site: schreiberNet.com Marla Schulman, Vice President Contact: Amanda Starley, Translator Resources

Founded 1984. Member: ATA. Uses freelance translators and interpreters. Accepts unsolicited resumes. Applicants should have appropriate linguistic and technical background, translation experience, current electronic equipment, and a track record of consistent timely delivery, accuracy and professional integrity. (Interpreters are judged on their track records and references.) Resumes are responded to with a questionnaire requesting more specific information and offering the option of completing a short written test. Returned questionnaires are carefully screened, and returned tests are carefully checked. If both are satisfactory, the candidate is given an opportunity to translate an actual assignment. Translates (both ways) mainly Japanese, Russian, German, French, Spanish, Chinese, Italian, Arabic, Korean, Vietnamese, Hebrew, Polish, and Dutch, and close to 90 additional languages and dialects. Emphasis on patents, aerospace, Law, Medicine, Communications, Computers, Engineering, Public Relations, Military and Maritime Subjects, Chemical Subjects, and Business and Finance. STI translates around 30 million words a year and maintains a pool of over 1300 translators - 350 active, and 200 of those very active. In addition to translation and interpretation, the company produces multilingual brochures and advertisements, prints manuals and business literature in a variety of multinational fonts, and does voice-overs for video and films. **Schreiber Publishing**, its newest division, was started in 1994 by STI's founder, Mordecai Schreiber. It publishes books (notably *The Translator's Handbook*) and produces support materials for translators.

Sebastian Lantos, LLC, 5111 East 89th Court, Tulsa, OK 74137 Phone:(918)481-1465 Fax: (918)481-0841 e-mail: language@gorilla.net
Web site: lantosconsulting.com Sebastian Lantos, Head Contact: Theresa Frescott, Office Manager
Founded 1996. Member: NAJIT. Uses freelance translators and interpreters. Accepts unsolicited resumes. Resumes are filed until needed. Main requirement for applicants is reliability. Translates mainly Spanish, French, Italian, Chinese, Japanese, and Russian. Also Korean, Vietnamese, and German. mains areas are medical, legal, and federal. Maintains a pool of 15 translators. The company also specializes in language tutoring, Hispanic personnel bilingual training.

SH3, Inc., 5338 East 115th St., Kansas City, MO 64137 Phone: (816)767-1117Fax:(816)767-1727 e-mail: inbox@sh3.com Web site: sh3.com Contact: Cathy Hubbard, General Manager
Founded 1980. Member: ATA, STC, EMI, NASM. Translates (both ways) mainly French, German, Italian, Spanish, Portuguese, Swedish, Chinese, and Japanese. Emphasis on Agricultural and Industrial Equipment, and Consumer Equipment translation. Prospective translators should have Windows-based computer, modem and fax; they should have experience in the agriculture, industrial and mechanical areas. Translator's Workbench is a definite plus. Resumes are reviewed by subject specialty, experience, and language, and flagged for a future contact. **SH3** maintains an active pool of 70 translators. Does around 20 million words a year. The company deals in high volume, highly technical manuals.

Speak Easy Languages, 757 South Main St., Plymouth, MI 48170 Phone:(734)459-5556 Fax:(734)459-1460 e-mail: selanguages@earthlink. net Contact: Cristina Clark
Founded 1980. Translates all major language pairs. Emphasis on Automotive business, Brochure, Advertising and Legal translation. Prospective translators should be ATA accredited and possess fax and modem capabilities. Resumes are filed and the applicant called upon as the circumstance arises. **Speak Easy** maintains a pool of 100 translators. The company also provides talent for voiceover work.

Spectrum Multilanguage Communications, 225 West 39th St., New York, NY 10018 Phone: (212)391-3940 Fax: (212)921-5246 e-mail: 76046.2123@compuserve.com Web site: come.to/spectrum Contact: Chiara Scandone, Language Resources Manager
Founded 1955. Member: ATA, DGA, IDIA. Translates Spanish, French, German, Italian, Japanese, Chinese, Russian, Arabic, Dutch and all major business languages from English. Emphasis on Marketing, Advertising, Packaging and Public Relations translation. Prospective translators should exhibit a high degree of competence, reliability, and excellent writing style. They should possess a modem, fax, and word processing capabilities. Resumes are reviewed by the language resources manager. **Spectrum** provides complete ad-quality in-house typesetting and color pre-press capabilities in virtually all languages and alphabets.

Superior Translations, a division of Toward, Inc., 1924 Minnesota Ave., Duluth, MN 55802 Phone: (218) 727-2572 Fax: (218)727-2653 e-mail: towardinc@aol.com Web site: interpretazioni.com Karla Ward, President Contact: Elisa Troiani, VP/Language Consultant

Founded 1993. Member: ATA. Uses freelance translators and interpreters. Accept unsolicited resumes. Resumes for translation and interpretation should be mailed. Applicants are carefully screened and required to submit samples, references, and times tests. Requirements are honesty, accuracy, editing/proofing skills, reason-able rates, punctuality, and an eye for detail. Translates mainly German, Spanish, Italian, French, Portuguese, Chinese, Japanese, Arabic, and Russian. Emphasis on all subject areas. Has 250-300 translators in its pool.

Sykes Enterprises, Incorporated, 5757 Central Ave., Ste. G, Boulder, CO 80301 Phone:(303)440-0909 Fax:(303)440-6369 e-mail: wpid@corp. sykes.com Web site: sykes.com Contact: Recruiting Coordinator, Worldwide Product Information Development

Sykes was founded in 1977; translation services started in 1989. Member: ATA, CTA, LISA, STC. Uses freelance translators and accepts unsolicited resumes. Looks for linguists specialized in localization. Requires native language ability. Prefers translation degree. Applicants are tested. Must have full PC processing and communication ability. Main languages are English into all major Asian, Middle Eastern, Latin American, and European languages. Main areas are software, hardware, on-line help, and documentation. **Sykes** is a large company which provides information support services. Language services are coordinated from Boulder, Colorado, Edinburgh, Scotland, and Leuven, Belgium.

-T-

Techno-Graphics and Translations, Inc., 1451 East 168th St., South Holland, IL 60473 Phone: (708)331-3333 Fax: (708)331-0003 e-mail: techno@wetrans4u.com Web site: wetrans4u.com David L. Bond, President Contact: Pinay Gaffney, Senior Project Manager

Founded 1972. Member: ATA. Uses freelance translators and interpreters. Accepts unsolicited resumes. Resumes are entered in database. Requires native ability and technical background. Translates (both ways) mainly European, Asian, and Middle Eastern languages. Main areas are telecommunications, agriculture, industry, automotive, and medical. Worldwide pool of 200 translators.

Toward, Inc., *see* **Superior Translations, a division of Toward, Inc.**

Tradux, 235 Montgomery, Ste. 1126, San Francisco, CA 94104 Phone: (415)982-8616 Fax: (415-982-8615 Contact: Xavier

Transimpex Translations, 8301 East 166th St., Belton, MO 64012 Phone: (816)561-3777 Fax:(816)561-5515 e-mail: transmpx@sound.net Web site: transimpex.com Brian U. White, Head Contact: Ingrid Pelger or Doris Ganser

Founded 1974. Member: ATA (Doris Ganser). Trade Club of Greater Kansas City. Uses freelance translators and interpreters. Accepts unsolicited resumes. Resumes are put in database until needed. Requires degree in linguistics or translation. Main languages translated are German, French, Spanish, Portuguese, Italian, Japanese, Russian, and Arabic. Translates all subjects, with long experience in "localization." Has overall pool of some 5000 translators, with about 150 active ones.

Translation Company of New York, Inc., 8 South Maple Ave., Marlton, NY 08053 Phone: (609)983-4733 Fax: (609)983-4595 e-mail: tcny@compuserve.com Contact: Betsy Lussi

Founded 1983. Member: ATA. Uses freelance translators and accepts unsolicited resumes. Main languages (both ways) are French, German, Italian, Spanish, Japanese, and Portuguese. Main areas are pharmaceutical, chemical, medical, engineering, and electronics. Does about 7-8 million words a year. Has active pool of 200 translators.

Translations Unlimited, 1455 Forest Hill SE, Grand Rapids, MI 49546 Phone: (616)942-5742 Fax: (616)957-8551 e-mail: lmathews@calvin.edu Contact: Leslie Mathews, Director

Founded 1980. Member: ATA. Uses freelance translators and interpreters. Accepts unsolicited resumes. Resumes are reviewed on a quarterly bases, filed, and used as needed. Applicants must be native speakers in target language, have experience, and be able to transmit text by e-mail. Main languages are French, Spanish, German, Japanese, Portuguese, Italian, and Vietnamese. Main areas are patents, sales literature, video scripts, and voice-overs, employee handbooks, sales literature, legal documents, and technical specifications. Translator pool of 25-30.

Translingua, PO Box 1662, Rancho Santa Fe, CA 92067 Phone: (619)259-5855 Fax: (619)259-9433 e-mail: nicole@translingua.com Web site: access-translingua.com Contact: Nicole Deuvaert, President
Founded 1976. Member: SD Chamber of Commerce. Ad Club of San Diego. SD Convention & Visitors Bureau. Uses freelance translators and interpreters. Accepts unsolicited resumes. Main languages (both ways) are Spanish, French, German, Japanese, Portuguese, Chinese, and Korean. Main areas are technical, biotech, electronic, medical, and legal. Has pool of some 500 translators.

Transperfect, 2536 Barstow Ave., Clovis, CA 93611 Phone: (554)323-8915 Fax: (554)298-8996 e-mail: mortrans@lightspeed.net Web site: thetranslators.com Contact: Morton S. Rothberg, CEO
Founded 1992. Member: ATA, Fresno Chamber of Commerce, SJVITA, Hispanic Chamber. Uses freelance translators and interpreters. Accepts unsolicited resumes. Resumes are classified, graded, and filed. Requires college degree with specific language native ability, computer, e-mail. Main languages are Spanish, French, Portuguese, German, Chinese, Japanese, and Arabic. Main areas are food industry and legal. Pool of 250 translators. Has affiliate offices in Europe, South America, and the Far East.

Transtek Associates, Inc., 599 North Avenue, Door 9, Wakefield, MA 01888 Phone: (781) 245-7980 Fax: (781)245-7993 e-mail: michle@transtekassociatesinc.com Web site: transtekassociatesinc.com Contact: Michele Phillips, President
Founded 1964. Uses freelance translators and interpreters. Accepts unsolicited resumes.

-U-

University Language Center, Inc., 1313 Fifth St. SE, Ste. 201, Minneapolis, MN 55414 Phone:(612)379-3574 Fax:(612)379-3832 e-mail: translation@ulanguage.com Web site: ulanguage.com Contact: Therese Shafranski, Translation Department Manager
Founded 1986. Member: ATA, The American Council on the Teaching of Foreign Languages, The Minnesota Council on the Teaching of Languages and Cultures, The International Alliance for Learning. Accepts resumes from translators and interpreters. Resumes are reviewed for language skills, areas of expertise, native language, relevant academic and professional work, hardware and softare capabilities, accreditations, awards, and professional or community involvement. Especially interested in formatting capabilities for non-Roman alphabets. Translates (both ways) Spanish, French, German, Italian, Portuguese, Russian, Chinese, Japanese and Hmong, as well as Turkish, Indonesian, Arabic and all Southeast Asian languages. Emphasis in all technical areas. Maintains a pool of 250 translators. The company handles all phases of production from translation to camera-ready art, including cultural assessment of the source documents.

-W-

WKI International Communications, 27 West 20th St., Ste. 402, New York, NY 10011 Phone: (212)255-6100 Fax: (212)255-8461 e-mail: 103153.3012@compuserve.com Contact: Koren Riesterer
Founded 1989. Member: ATA. Translates Spanish, Portuguese, French, German, Italian, Chinese, Japanese and all other major languages, both from and into English. Emphasis on Advertising, Financial, Legal, Marketing, Technical, and General Business translation. Prospective translators should be ATA accredited, native speakers of the target language, and experts in specific technical areas. Resume receipt is confirmed by phone and the resumes kept on file according to the applicant's qualifications. The company focuses on the adaptation and graphic production of business communications materials. They are also looking for experienced proofreaders with a sensitivity to graphic treatments.

WORDNET, Inc., 30 Nagog Park, PO Box 2255, Acton, MA 01720-6255 Phone: (978)264-0600 Fax:(978)263-3839 e-mail: wordnet@wordnet.com Web site: wordnet.com Lee Chadeayne, President Contact:Stephanie Hooker, Marketing Manager

Founded 1985. Member: ATA, German-American Business Council. Uses freelance translators and interpreters. Accepts unsolicited resumes. Resumes are reviews and applicants are sent out forms to fill out, and are periodically tested and evaluated. Main languages translated are French, Spanish, German, Italian, Chinese, Japanese, and Korean. Main areas are technical, medical, machinery, legal, and business/marketing. Maintains a pool of some 2000 translators. The company specializes in translation, typesetting and printing, preparing brochures, catalogs, manuals, legal agreements and Web pages.They help companies get started in the international marketplace.

Worldwide Translations, Inc., 1 Warren Way, Amherst, NH 03031 Phone: (800)293-0412 Fax:(603)672-5574 e-mail: wwtrans @compu-serve.com Web site: wwtranslations.com Contact: Robert Sansing, President

Founded 1992. Member: ATA, RAPS. Translates German, French, Spanish, Italian, Swedish, Dutch, Japanese, Portuguese, Greek and Danish, both from and into English. Emphasis on Medical, Machinery Manufacture and Computer Products translation. Prospective translators should be native-speaking ATA members with 3+ years technical translation experience and references. Resumes are responded to by telephone when work becomes available. **Worldwide** maintains a pool of 50 translators. The company is expert in the CE Mark and Medical Device areas and specializes in the translation of instructional manuals. They hold their translators to a high standard of accuracy.

APPENDIX F: TRAINING PROGRAMS FOR TRANSLATORS

Academic programs for those interested in translation and interpretation are in a state of flux. There is a growing recognition of the fact that the most critical need for the practicing translator is hands-on experience, although some of the policymakers in academia continue to cling to theory rather than practice. Programs are growing and expanding, to include many new areas. If interested in an academic program, contact one or more of the following schools and find out more about their latest offerings.

As with the Translation Agency listings in Appendix 4, detailed information in the following entries is the result of responses to an information questionnaire sent to the various schools. The quantity of such information is based on those responses and does not reflect any value judgment on the part of the editors.*

UNITED STATES

ARKANSAS
University of Arkansas, Fayetteville, AR 72701
Web site: uark.edu
Literary translation program.

CALIFORNIA
The Graduate School of Translation & Interpretation Studies, Monterey Institute of International Studies, 425 Van Buren St., Monterey, CA 93940 Phone: (831)647-4170 Fax:(831)647-3560 e-mail: ddeterra@miis.edu Web site: miis.edu/gsti/gsti.html Contact: Dr. Diane de Terra
Now in its thirtieth year, the school offers an MA degree in Chinese, French, German, Japanese, Korean, Spanish, Russian, and English Translation. All major technical areas of translation are taught, including computer-assisted translation, software localization, terminology, and the business of translation. The School also offers an MA in Interpreting— Simultaneous, Consecutive and Conference. Students must have a BA with a 3.0 GPA and a TOEFL of 600+, as well as study abroad and GRE. The Graduate School is an independent entity within the Monterey Institute. The School also offers Certificates to students lacking a BA, but who demonstrate the necessary level of language proficiency.

San Diego State University, Department of Spanish & Portuguese Languages & Literatures, 5402 College Ave., San Diego, CA 92182
Phone: (619)594-6588 Fax:(619)594-5293 e-mail: gsegade@mail. sdsu. edu Web site: sdsu.edu
Contact: Dr. Gustavo V. Segade, Director of Translation Studies
SDSU's Translation program has been in place sixteen years. The University offers Certificates in Translation Studies and in Court Interpreting in Spanish< >English. Translation covers all major tech-nical areas; Interpreting is Legal only. Students must have advanced Spanish grammar or equivalent courses, and must pass a proficiency examination in English. There are five courses in Translation and six in Court Interpreting, including an internship. The University also provides training for State and Federal accreditation examinations in Court Interpreting.

Stanford University, Stanford, CA 94305 (415) 497-1068 Web site: stanford.edu
Certificate Program in Translation and Interpretation.

University of California, Los Angeles, 10995 Le Conte Ave., Los Angeles, CA 90024
Certificate in Interpretation and Translation in Spanish.

California State University, Long Beach, 1250 Bellflower Blvd, Long Beach, CA 90840 Phone:
(916)278-6011 Web site: csulb.edu.
BA in Spanish translation.

California State University, Sacramento, 6000 J St., Sacramento, CA 95819
Courses in translation and interpretation.

Fuller Theological Seminary, 135 N. Oakland Ave., Pasadena, CA 91182
Translation concentration in graduate degrees.

San Jose State University, Department of Foreign Languages, One Washington Sq., San Jose,
CA 95192-0091 Phone: (408)924-4602 Fax:(408)924-4607 e-mail: msigler@jsuvm.sjsu.edu
Contact: Dr. M. del Carmen Sigler, Chair
Although **SJSU** offers courses in Chinese, French, German, Greek, Hebrew, Italian, Japanese,
Latin, Portuguese, Russian and Spanish, its Translation offerings are limited to one introductory
course—"Basics of Translation"—in Spanish only. The course has been offered for several years.
It is considered an elective in the Bachelor's Degree in Spanish program.The prerequisite for the
course is the attainment of an advanced level in the study of Spanish. The course deals with texts
from most major technical areas. **SJSU** plans to offer more courses in translation in the future, at
least one of which will be at the MA level.

CONNECTICUT
Wesleyan University, Middleton, CT 06457
Interpreters for the Deaf Workshop

DISTRICT OF COLUMBIA
Gallaudet College, Department of ASL, Linguistics and Interpretation, 800 Florida Ave., NE,
Washington, DC 20002 Phone: (202)651-5450 Fax: (202)651-5741 Web site: gallaudet.edu
Contact: Dr. Michael Kemp
Only liberal arts college exclusively for the deaf. Offers Master's degree in ASL.

Georgetown University, 1221 36th St. N.W., Washington, DC 20057
Certificate of Proficiency as Conference Interpreter, and Certificate in Translation in French,
Spanish, German, Italian, and Portuguese.

The American University, Department of Language & Foreign   Studies, 4400 Massachusetts
Ave., NW, Washington, DC 20016
Phone: (202)885-2381 Fax: (202)885-1076Web site: american.edu/lfs
Contact: Consuelo Gall

The American University's translation program has been operating for 13 years. It teaches French, Spanish, Russian and German translation, with an emphasis on translation into English. Students are required to have completed the third-year level of their language. Courses cover general translation, covering a variety of areas including business, literature, journalism, etc. Students are awarded a certificate on completion of the course. Study materials vary with the language. There is no interpreter training.

FLORIDA

Florida International University, Department of Modern Languages University Park Campus, Miami, FL 33199 Phone: (305)348-2851 Fax: (305)348-1085 voice mail: (305)348-2049 Contact: Dr. Leonel A. de la Cuesta, Director Translation-Interpretation Program
FIU's Translation-Interpretation Program has been in operation since 1980. It teaches Translation primarily in Spanish< >English, with some French as well. The program awards Certificates in Translation Studies and Legal Translation. The University also offers Simultaneous and Consecutive (but not Conference) Interpreter training in English< >Spanish and awards a Certificate in Court Interpreting. Students are required to have at least two years of college education and must be bilingual. Studies cover most major areas of technical translation (Legal, Medical, Business, Technological-Scientific, Literary, Journalism, Publishing, etc.).The University also provides support training for practicing translators and interpreters who want to strengthen their skills in the field.

Florida Atlantic University, Department of Languages and Linguistics, 777 Glades Rd., Boca Raton, FL 33431-0991 Phone: (561)297-3864 Fax: (561)297-2657 email: gosser@fau.edu Contact: Mary Ann Gosser-Esquilín, Head of Spanish Programs
Fourth-year level course in Spanish translation that draws on Jack Child's *Introduction to Spanish Translation*; no specialized translation program.

Florida A&M University, Office of International Services and Summer Sessions, Translation and Critical Languages Center, 304 Perry Paige N., Tallahassee, FL 32307 Phone: (904) 561-2482 Contact: Dr. Eva. C. Wanton, Associate Vice President for Academic Affairs.
Florida A&M's translation program has been operating for ten years, and offers a B.A. in Spanish and French and a minor in these degree programs. Instruction in German, Chinese, Japanese and other languages on request is also available. Prerequisites for the program include successful completion of a written entrance exam and an oral proficiency interview. The program teaches courses in Legal, Medical, Business, Scientific and Educational translation. Training materials include journals, newspapers, magazines and textbooks. Successful completion of the program requires 18 semester hours of translations and an internship at an overseas translation institute, as well as written and oral exit examinations.

GEORGIA

Georgia State University, Department of Modern and Classical Languages, 1 University Plaza, Atlanta, GA 30303 Phone: (404)651-2265 Fax: (404)651-1785 Contact: Dr. James Murray
Georgia State University's Certificate in Translation and Interpretation Program has been in operation since 1979. It teaches French, German and Spanish translation. Students must pass an entrance examination and possess a baccalaureate degree. They are advised to acquire typing and word-processing skills prior to registration. Courses cover advanced techniques in both general

and technical translation, as well as the pro-fessional aspects of translation and interpretation. The Interpretation program provides professional training in simultaneous and consecutive interpreting in French and Spanish. Applicants must have completed the Translation program or be able to demonstrate equivalent skills. The Spanish program includes a course emphasizing court interpretation.

HAWAII
University of Hawaii, Manoa, East-West Rd., Bldg 1, Rm 6, Honolulu, HI 96822
Certificate in conference interpretation.

IDAHO
College of Southern Idaho, PO Box 1238, Twin Falls, ID 83303 Phone: (208) 733-9554

IOWA
University of Iowa, English Department, 308 EPB, Iowa City, IA 52242
Master's degree in literary translation.

ILLINOIS
University of Illinois at Urbana-Champaign, 707 S. Mathews St., Urbana, IL 61801
Courses in Russian literary translation.

INDIANA
Indiana University, University Budget Office, Bryan Hall 115, Bloomington, IN 47405 Phone: (812)855-6818 Fax: (812)855-8990 Web site: indiana.edu/complit/trans.html Contact: See individual language
Indiana U. has been offering a literary translation program for about 20 years. The school teaches about 26 languages, from Arabic to Zulu. Courses include the theory and practice of literary translation, which have resulted in some highly-regarded translations from Chinese, French, German, Greek, Italian, Japanese, Romanian, and Spanish, among others.

KANSAS
Kansas State University, Department of Modern Languages, 104 Eisenhower Hall, Manhattan, KS 66506-1003 Phone: (785)532-1988 Fax: (785)532-7004 e-mail: bradshaw@ksu.edu Contact: Dr. Bradley A. Shaw, Associate Professor
Kansas State teaches Spanish, French, German, Japanese, Russian, Italian, Arabic and Latin. Although there is no translation program, KSU offers an Introduction to Spanish Translation course, designed for upper level undergraduates and graduate students. It features bi-directional exercises, a variety of texts, and a discussion of professional issues. A second Spanish as well as a French course are being prepared.

Johnson County Community College, College Blvd. at Quivira Rd., Overland Pass, KS 66210

MARYLAND
University of Maryland, French and Italian Department, 3106 Jimenez Hall, College Park, MD 20742 Phone: (301)405-4024 Fax: (301)314-9928
Translation courses in French and Italian. Subjects covered are literary, journalistic, commercial,

and political. There are about four courses in French at the undergraduate level that deal with translation. Two of these focus on business French. There is also a French translation course at the graduate level. One undergraduate course in Italian deals with literary translation.

MASSACHUSETTS
Bentley College, Legal and Medical Interpreter Certificate Program, 175 Forest St., Waltham, MA 02452-4705 Phone: (781)891-2868 Fax: (781)891-3449 Web site: bentley.edu e-mail: fsalimbene@Bentley.edu Contact: Franklyn P. Salimbene, Director
Bentley's Legal and Medical Interpreter Program was initiated in September 1996. The program offers Spanish- and Portuguese-speaking students a certificate in Legal or Medical Interpretation. The program includes instruction in written translation, and both simultaneous and consecutive interpreting, as well as in specialized vocabularies and standards of practice. Applicants must be bilingual and must have completed a minimum of 14 years of education, including two years of college or its equivalent, and must pass an entrance examination. The course employs instructor-developed materials and exercises, numerous dictionaries and a few standard texts.

Brandeis University, Interdisciplinary Program of Literary Studies, Shiffman 108, MS 024, Waltham, MA 02254-9110 Phone: (781)736-3200 Fax: (781)736-3207 e-mail: european@binah.cc.brandeis.edu Contact: Luis Yglesias, Chair
Brandeis' Translation Program has been in operation for three years. The University awards both MAs and Certificates in Translation in French, German, Italian, Hebrew, Russian and Spanish (both European and Latin American). Students are required to have a Bachelor's degree or equivalent, must submit a statement of purpose, and must display evidence of strong competence in both English and the language of proficiency. The program provides professional training in literary translation. It combines seminars in theory with courses in literary study and practice translation texts. Certificate requires eight courses. MA program includes a translation project with an introduction and critical apparatus. *The program was suspended for 1999.*

Elms College, Chicopee, MA 01013
French and Spanish translation courses.

University of Massachusetts, Room 608, Goodell, Amherst, MA 01003 Contact: Fran Fortino
U-Mass is in the process of putting into place a Translation program. The result will be an MA in Translation.

MICHIGAN
Marygrove College, 8425 West McNichols Rd., Detroit, MI 48221-2599 Phone: (313)862-8000, ex.374 Fax: (313)864-6670 Contact: Dr. Karen Davis
Marygrove's Translation Program has been in operation since 1974. It teaches Literary, Legal, Medical, Scientific and Commercial Translation in French and Spanish. The program awards a Certificate of Achieve-ment for the completion of three separate workshops. The College also offers training in consecutive interpretation in French and Spanish. Students are required to have four semesters of college-level work in French or Spanish. The third workshop features an independent project chosen by the student, following guidelines set by the ATA and the MLA (Modern Language Association).

Western Michigan University, Kalamazoo, MI 49008 Web site:wmich. edu
Technical translation courses.

MINNESOTA
St. Olaf College, Northfield, MN 55057
Courses in translation.

MISSOURI
Washington University, St. Louis, MO 63130
Courses in literary translation.

NEBRASKA
University of Nebraska at Kearney, Kearney, NE 68849 Phone: (308)865-8493 Fax: (308)865-8806 e-mail: bbt@unk.edu Contact: Dr. Betty Becker-Theye, Director, Program in Translation/Interpretation
U-Nebraska at Kearney's Translation/Interpretation program has been in operation for 21 years. Under the ægis of Modern Languages, the program offers both BAs and certificates in French and Spanish Translation and Interpretation. Students are required to demonstrate proficiency or successfully accomplish senior-level language studies. Both literary and nonliterary translation are taught. Students who complete the program are ready for graduate studies, and in some cases, professional employment as translators and/or interpreters.

NEVADA
University of Nevada, Reno, NV 89557
Court Interpreter Seminar/Workshops

NEW JERSEY
Montclair State University, Department of French, German and Russian, Upper Montclair, NJ 07043 Phone: (201)655-5145 e-mail: oppenheim@mail.montclair.edu Contact: Dr. Lois Oppenheim
Montclair State's Translation program has been in operation for twenty-six years. It concentrates in French, German, and Spanish. The Uni-versity offers both Certificates and BAs. It teaches Scientific, Economic, Legal, and Literary Translation. Specific areas vary from semester to semester. There is also one course in Interpreting (Simultaneous, Consecutive and Conference) for French- and Spanish-language students. Students must be at least Juniors majoring in their language. They are required to do an individual long translation in their Senior year. The program prepares students for career opportunities in the NY/NJ metropolitan area, in industry and commerce, advertising and tourism, and governmental services. Students are encouraged to double-major in a technical speciality.

Rutgers, the State University, Department of Spanish and Portuguese, 105 George St., New Brunswick, NJ 08901-1414 Phone: (732)932-9412 x25 Fax: (732)932-9837 e-mail: zatlin@rci.rutgers.edu Contact: Prof. Phyllis Zatlin
Rutgers has been offering a Spanish translation program for 20 years. In 1987, an M.A. option was added, along with a certificate in translation. Requirements include proficiency at native or

near-native level in Spanish and English. Areas covered are legal, technical, literary, and other subjects. There is also simultaneous and consecutive interpreter training in Spanish. The program also offers an internship in translation and interpretation.

NEW YORK
Columbia University, Barnard College, 3009 Broadway, New York, NY 10027
BA in literary translation.

Binghamton University (SUNY),Translation Research and Instruction Program, PO Box 6000, Binghamton, NY 13902-6000 Phone: (607)777- 6726 Fax: (607)777-2280 e-mail: trip@binghamton.edu Web site: trip. binghamton.edu
Contact: Professor Marilyn Gaddis Rose, Director
SUNY-Binghamton's Translation Research and Instruction Program is an autonomous graduate teaching unit, not affiliated with any departments in the University. The program has been operating since January 1971. Languages offered are Arabic, French, Chinese, Spanish, German, Japanese, Korean, Portuguese, Italian, Russian and Modern Greek. The University offers Graduate Certificates incorporated into a Master's or Doctoral degree. Students must have high fluency in their source language and effective expression in their target language. Emphasis is literary and scholarly translation, with generalist studies scheduled for January 1998. Management of terminology data bases is also taught. Study materials include *Translation Horizons*. There is no Interpreter training.

Brooklyn College, 2900 Bedford Ave., Brooklyn, NY 11210
Translation courses.

City University of New York, 33 W. 42nd St., New York, NY 10036
MA in translation.

Fordham College, Fordham Rd., Bronx, NY 10458
Courses in translation.

Hofstra University, Hempstead, NY 11550
translation courses.

New York University, School of Continuing Education & Professional Studies, Foreign Languages Translation Studies, 48 Cooper Sq., Rm 107, New York, NY 10003 Phone: (212)998-7028 Fax: (212)995-4139 e-mail: lat4@is7.nyu.edu Contact: Lorena Terando, Translation Studies Coordinator.
NYU's Translation program has been in operation for 15 years. It offers translation certificates in English > Spanish, English > Portuguese, English, French > English, German > English on site, and English > Spanish on line, as well as English < > Spanish court interpreting. The program emphasizes legal, commercial, medical, and technical translation with elective courses available in marketing, literary and terminology/
database management, among others. Since it is a hands-on, intensive translator and interpreter training program, students translate "real-life" texts in the Translation program, and use language labs in the Court Interpreting program. In addition, a wide variety of internships is available.

Students must pass an entrance exam to prove proficiency in both target and source languages. They must maintain a B or better average and complete the program within four years.

State University of New York at Albany, 1400 Washington Ave., Albany, NY 12222
Certificate in Russian translation.

NORTH CAROLINA
University of North Carolina at Charlotte, Charlotte, NC 28223
German translation program.
North Carolina State University at Raleigh, Foreign Languages, Box 8106, Raleigh, NC 27695

NORTH DAKOTA
North Dakota State University, Fargo, ND 58105
Translation courses.

OHIO
Kent State University, Kent, OH 44242
MA in French, German and Spanish translation.

Ohio State University, 1841 Millikin Rd., Columbus, OH 43210
BA in Russian translation.

Notre Dame College, 4545 College Rd., Cleveland, OH 44121
Translation program.

Antioch College, Japan Program, Yellow Springs, OH 45387 Phone: (513)767-7331 Fax: (513)767-6469 Contact: Harold Wright, Professor of Japanese
Antioch offers courses in Japanese, Spanish, German, and French translation into English. Although there is no specific Translation program, the College does offer a workshop in poetry translation. Students are required to know the source and target languages in order to take this course.

Baldwin-Wallace College, Berea, OH 44017
Translation courses.

Bowling Green State University, Bowling Green, OH 43403
Translation courses.

Wright State University, Colonel Glenn Hwy, Dayton, OH 45435
Translation courses.

OKLAHOMA
Tulsa Community College, International Language Center, 6111 E. Skelly Dr., Tulsa, OK 74135 Phone: (918)595-7851 Fax: (918)595-7910 email: lwalker@vm.cc.tulsa.ok.us Contact:

Dr. Laura Walker, Director
Tulsa Community College requires four semesters within the target language before accepting undergraduate students into its specialized translation program which offers both Spanish and French. Students are introduced to the basic concepts and responsibilities related to translating. Instructor handouts and specialized documents provide practice with various types of materials. The result is an Associate degree.

PENNSYLVANIA
Carnegie-Mellon University, Department of Modern Languages, Baker Hall 160, Schenley Park, Pittsburgh, PA 15213-3890 Phone: (412)268-2934 Fax: (412)268-1328 e-mail: grtucker+@andrew.cmu.edu Contact: Professor G. Richard Tucker, Head, Department of Modern Languages
Carnegie-Mellon teaches French, German, Japanese, Russian, Spanish, Mandarin Chinese and Italian, but does not offer a specialized Translation program.

Mt. Aloysius Junior College, William Penn Hwy. Rte. 22, Cresson, PA 16630
Associate degree in interpreter training.

Pennsylvania State University, University Park, PA 16802
Graduate translation degree.

University of Pittsburgh, Language Learning Resource Center, Pittsburgh, PA 15260 Phone: (412)624-5900 Fax: (412)624-6793 e-mail: ptoth+@pitt.edu. Contact: Dr. Paul D. Toth
The University of Pittsburgh's Translation Program offers a certificate in Spanish, French, German and Italian into English translation in the commercial, legal, medical, business (general), and technical fields. Students must have at least a third-year-level of proficiency in their language. It takes on the average 3-4 semesters to complete the program. The university does not offer Interpreter training.

Immaculata College, Office #4, Faculty Center, Immaculata, PA 19345
Translation courses.

La Salle University, Philadelphia, PA 19141
Translation courses.

PUERTO RICO
University of Puerto Rico, Río Piedras campus Contact: Dr. Marshall Morris
M.A. in Translation.

RHODE ISLAND
University of Rhode Island, Kingston, RI 02881
Translation courses.

SOUTH CAROLINA
Lander College, Greenwood, SC 29646
Translation courses.

TENNESSEE

Chattanooga State Technical Community College, 4501 Amnicola Highway, Chattanooga, TN 37406
Offers associate degree in interpreter training.

Maryville College, Maryville, TN 37801

TEXAS

University of Texas at El Paso, El Paso, TX 79968
Minor in translation.

University of Texas at Arlington, 7500 W. Camp Wisdom Rd., Dallas, TX 75236
Courses in translation.

Southern Methodist University, Dallas, TX 75275
Courses in translation.

Texas Tech University, Lubbock, TX 79409
French translation courses.

University of Texas at Austin, Spanish & Portuguese Department, Austin, TX 78712 Phone: (512)471-4936 Fax: (512)471-8073 e-mail: fhensey@utxvms.cc.utexas.edu Contact: Professor Fritz Hensey or Madeline Sutherland-Meier (Department Head)
Austin's Translation program started in Fall 1996. The University offers selected courses as part of an interdepartmental MA in Translation under the ægis of Foreign Language Education. Program emphasis is mostly on literary translation. There is also a general introductory course in Consecutive Spanish< >English Interpreting.

UTAH

Brigham Young University, Provo, UT 84602
BA in Spanish translation.

Utah State University, Languages and Philosophy, 0720 Old Main Hill, Logan, UT 84322-0720 (435)797-1209 Fax: (435)797-1329 e-mail: Web site: usu.edu/~langphil Contact: Dr. Diane P. Michelfelder
USU's has offered a translation course in German, "Techniques in Translating German Texts," since 1984, covering the literary and general scientific fields. The course in not being offered at present.

VIRGINIA

George Mason University, Fairfax, VA 22030 Web Site: gmu.edu
Graduate certificate program in translation.

WASHINGTON

Translation and Interpretation Institute (in partnership with Bellevue Community College),

Academic Affairs Office, 2224 W. Viewmont Way West, Seattle, WA 98199 Phone: (206)281-9612 Fax: (206)284-2245 email: gls_csr@compuserve.com Contact: Courtney Searls-Ridge, Academic Director

T&I Institute has been in operation since 1994, with Translation programs in Spanish, German, Japanese, French, Russian, and Vietnamese, with other languages being offered according to demand. The program awards a certificate, with college credit also available. The course covers basic Translation skills. Students must show a high proficiency in their working languages. T&I also awards a certificate in Simultaneous and Consecutive Interpreting skills. Courses at T&I include advanced workshops, training in ethics and business practices, and courses dealing with technology and terminology management.

University of Washington, 5001 25th Ave., NE, Seattle, WA 98195
Translation courses.

WISCONSIN
North Central Technical Institute, 1000 Schonfield Ave., Wausau, WI 54401
Program for Interpreters.

CANADA

BRITISH COLUMBIA
Langara College, Department of Modern Languages, 100 West 49th Ave., Vancouver, BC V5Y 2Z6, CANADA Phone: (604)323-5282 Fax: (604)323-5555 e-mail: dyada@langara.bc.ca Contact: Dorothy Yada, Department Chair

Langara offers courses in French, Spanish, German, Japanese and Chinese, but does not have a Translation program.

ONTARIO
Laurentian University, Department of French Studies and Translation, 935 Ramsey Lake Rd., Sudbury, Ontario P3E 2C6, CANADA Phone: (705)675-1151 Fax: (705)675-4885 e-mail: bdubeprevost@nickel.laurentian.ca Web site:laurentian.ca/www.francais Ronald Henry, Chairman

The English-French translation program is 31 years old. Degree offered is Bachelor of Science in Languages (B.S.L.) Applicants must have solid background in English and French, and take a writing competence test in both languages. The program covers general, business-commercial, scientific, and technical translation. Simultaneous and consecutive interpretation are also taught.

University of Ottawa School of Translation & Interpretation, PO Box 450, Station A, Ottawa, Ontario K1N 6N5, CANADA Contact: Dr. Annie Brisset

APPENDIX G: THE INTERNET

The Internet has opened up opportunities for translators as never before in human history. The translation field has become increasingly "wired," witnessing a proliferation of sites relating to professional activities, job-hunting, commercial products, and online reference materials for translators. It is not an exaggeration to say that translators do themselves (and potentially their clients) quite a disservice by ignoring the virtual translation community.

This section will introduce you to a selection of highly-regarded and well-maintained sites of use to translators. It assumes basic Web literacy; if you are not familiar with how to use the Internet, there are innumerable Web-related "how to" books available. Your public library can help you get started (and, in many cases, provide free access to online services). Of course, the Internet's ever-changing nature guarantees that certain Web sites will decline or disappear, while new ones will emerge by the time this book becomes available. So please be aware that you will probably have to do some updating of the following information on your own.

Where We Are on the Web

First, let us invite you to Schreiber Publishing's Web site. Our address: **schreiberNet.com**. It first went online in March 1996. Its objective is to provide reference literature, training materials, and useful information for translators. We fully intend to keep expanding it, and we hope all translators will benefit from it.

Professional Activities

Translators wishing to learn about the state of their profession will benefit from a visit to the American Translators Association's site, **atanet.org**. I discuss the ATA in greater detail in the chapter on Translators' Organizations; its Web site includes information on the Association's formal activities such as conferences, publications and accreditation procedures. Even if you are not an ATA member, the site is useful because it can guide you to other translation-related sites.

Another major web-site of interest to translators is the site of the international umbrella organization of the world's translator associations, the International Federation of Translators, found on **fit-ift.org**

Aquarius, at **aquarius.net.** Claims to be "the most comprehensive and the largest interactive database of translators and interpreters on the WorldWideWeb." This commercial web site lists translation agencies seeking translators and interpreters who, in turn, can post resumes to make their services known. It also links to other translation sites.

Networking with Other Translators

An extremely popular program on the Internet for translators has been the *Language Forum* of CompuServe, popularly known as FLEFO (Foreign Language Education Forum). You have to subscribe to this forum to be able to participate. You enter FLEFO in the keyword box and you find yourself in a virtual forum full of translators from around the world, who post messages and get answers to almost any question a translator may ask, from the cost of a dictionary, to the meaning of a word, to a social get-together. FLEFO can also link you to translation Web sites.

Another online forum for translators is the newsgroup: subscribers post messages and receive answers (say, to a specialized translation query). A newsgroup for translators is sci.lang. translation.

Reference Materials

The Translator's Home Companion at **rahul.net/lai/ companion. html**, provides Links to glossaries, dictionaries, translation publications, and other translators.
The Interpreters' Network at **terpsnet.com** lists resources and topics of interest to interpreters.

The Human Languages Page at **june29.com/HLP/** provides links to other translation-related sites, including some listed here.
Language Today, an online publication (also available in print; see Bibliography appendix) covering language technology, translation and interpreting: **logos.it/language_today**

Online Dictionary Services

Eurodicautom at **europa.eu.int/comm/sdt/edic/** is a very useful service, Eurodicautom handles European languages such as Spanish, Portuguese, French, German, Italian, English, Danish and Dutch. Includes many specialized dictionaries in non-technical, legal and technical areas. Terms are both translated and defined.
Online Dictionaries (Bucknell) at **bucknell.edu/~rbeard/ diction. html** covers a far greater range of languages than the above entry. It provides links to dictionaries and translations in many specializations.
Paderborn at **math-www.uni-paderborn.de/HTML/ Dictionaries. html** provides a list of dictionaries and links to vast numbers of specialized/multilingual dictionaries.

Glossaries

There are many mediocre glossaries out there in cyberspace, so use caution with this type of online resource. Here are some better ones:
refer.fr/termisti/liste.htm
yahoo.com/references/dictionaries
U.S. Government agencies provide some very useful glossaries. For example:
epa.gov (for environmental terminology).

General Language-Related Links

ranchopark.com/translatorlinks.html
http://polyglot.lss.wisc.edu/lss/lang/langlink.html

Finding Cultural Information

A quick way to access cultural and historical information on other countries is via The Electronic Embassy at **embassy.org.** This service provides links to embassy and/or United Nations home pages of many nations. Most countries' pages include links to cultural resources such as online newspapers, libraries, and so on. You may have to do some digging to find the information you're after, but if it exists online, you will probably find it by starting here. Also the foreign ministries of various countries are a good source for all sorts of information related to that particular country.

Other Basic Online Reference Sources

Worldwide phone directory: **Four11.com**
U.S. phone guide: **switchboard.com**
Guide to literature on the Internet: **http://books.mirror.org/gb. faraday.html**
World Fact Book: **http://dutettq.et.tudelft.nl/~koen/links/ worldfactbook. html**
Encyclopedia Britannica: **eb.com**

Shopping for Dictionaries

A prime source for dictionaries is i.b.d. Ltd.'s website:
ibdltd.com. It lists dictionaries in well over 100 languages, although it is looking to limit its operations.
Another site under construction is: **schoenhofs.com**.
Major virtual bookstores also have good selections of dictionaries (see box). Examples:
barnesandnoble.com
amazon.com
borders.com

You may also wish to consult these web sites of major dictionary publishers:

Elsevier at **elsevier.com**
Routledge at **routledge.com**
McGraw-Hill at **mcgraw-hill.com**

Need Spanish medical dictionaries? Here is a sample of our search results on the web-site **amazon.com** (19 items were shown):

Delmar's English/Spanish Pocket Dictionary for Health Professionals -
Usually ships in 24 hours
    Rochelle K. Kelz / Paperback / Published 1997
    Our Price: $23.95
    Read more about this title. . .

Diccionario de Terminos Medicos; Ingles-Espanol, Espanol-ingles -
Usually ships in 2-3 days
    Erich Ruiz Albrecht, Francisco Ruiz Albrecht / Hardcover / Published 1999
    Our Price: $80.50 - You Save: $34.50 (30%)

English and Spanish Medical Words and Phrases -
Usually ships in 24 hours
    Springhouse Publishing Co. Staff(Editor) / Paperback / Published 1998
    Our Price: $24.95

English-Spanish/Spanish-English Medical Dictionary = Diccionario Medico Ingles-Espanol Espanol-ingles : Diccionario Medico, Ingles-Espanol, Espanol-in - Usually ships in 24 hours
    Glenn T. Rogers(Editor) / Paperback / Published 1997
    Our Price- $15.96 - You Save: $3.99 (20%)
    Read more about this title...

Quick Order Form

Fax orders: (301) 424-2336. Send this form.

Telephone orders: Call 1 (800) 822-3213
(in Maryland: 301-424-7737 ext. 28)

E-mail orders: spbooks@aol.com.

Mail orders to: Schreiber Publishing, 51 Monroe St.,
Suite 101, Rockville MD 20850 USA

Please send the following books, programs, and/or a free catalog. I understand that I may return any of them for a full refund, for any reason, no questions asked:

❑ **The Translator's Self-Training Program** (circle the language/s of your choice):

Spanish   French   German   Japanese   Chinese   Italian   Portuguese   Russian   Arabic   Hebrew

(U.S. - $69.00 Abroad - $89)

❑ **The Translator's Self-Training Program** -
Advanced Spanish Legal Translation (U.S. $89 Abroad - $109)
Advanced Spanish Medical Translation (U.S. $89 Abroad - $109)

❑ **Multicultural Spanish Dictionary** - How Spanish Differs from Country to Country (U.S. $24.95 Abroad -$36)

❑ **American English Compendium** - The "Odds and Ends" of American English Usage (U.S. $19.95 Abroad $28)

❑ **The Translator's Handbook** 3rd Revised Edition - The leading guide for translators (U.S. $24.95 Abroad - $36)

❑ **Dictionary of Medicine** French-English (U.S. $179.50 Abroad - $199.50)

Name: _____

Address: _____

City: _____ State: _____ Zip: _____

Telephone: _____ e-mail: _____

Sales tax: Please add 5% sales tax in Maryland
Shipping (est.): $4 for the first book and $2.00 for each additional product
International: $ $9 for the first book, and $5 for each additional book

Payment: ❑ Cheque   ❑ Credit card: ❑ Visa   ❑ MasterCard

Card number:

Name on card: _____ Exp. Date: ____/____

Schreiber Publishing—The Translator's Best Friend©